Please Don't Lose the Date Card

KNIT YOUR OWN

DOVER PUBLICATIONS, Inc./New York

NORWEGIAN SWEATERS

complete
instructions for
50 authentic
sweaters,
hats, mittens,
gloves, caps, etc.

by DALE YARN COMPANY

This Dover edition, first published in 1974, is an expanded and revised version of the 1966 edition of "Knit it Yourself" published by J. W. Cappelens Forlag in Oslo, Norway. A new introduction and a list of sources of supply have been especially prepared for this edition.

International Standard Book Number: 0-486-23031-7
Library of Congress Catalog Card Number: 73-94350

Manufactured in the United States of America
Dover Publications, Inc.
180 Varick Street
New York, N. Y. 10014

INTRODUCTION

Making one's own clothes has never been as exciting and popular as it is today. Nor has there ever been such a wide variety of gay, imaginative and artistic patterns at the disposal of those who wish to express their own personality. It is no exaggeration to say that Norwegians are leaders in the field of creative handicrafts.

In the old days a great number of crafts were plied in the rural homesteads of Norway. There was no machinery to rely on; everything people needed for their daily life—farming and fishing implements, kitchen utensils and clothes—they fashioned themselves. Their work was utilitarian and artless at first, but as time went by the most exquisite objects began to appear, in wood-carving, rose-painting, weaving and knitting.

Knitting has always been essential to Norwegians for they required warm clothes in the bitterly

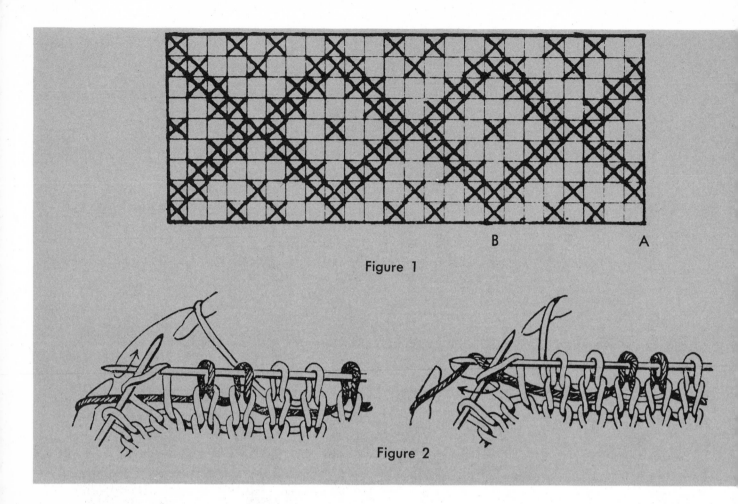

Figure 1

Figure 2

cold winters. The Norwegian farmer had wool, and he could card and spin. He had also acquired the art of making beautiful dyes from moss and other plants. With his needles and wool, he could now knit, not merely warm clothing, but garments of handsome design in brilliant colors for festive occasions. And so the handicraft of knitting patterns was born, steeped in the influence of the countryside and the national temperament. This handicraft thrives today as it did hundreds of years ago.

Originally the townsman frowned upon the idea of walking the streets in thick hand-knitted garments, and so the home craft was plied mainly in the rural districts. Today, however, fashion and sport call for these hand-knitted garments, and they are in greater demand than ever before.

This book contains directions for making a number of colorful knit garments, most of them based on old Norwegian patterns. The directions call for the use of Heilo Yarn, a four-ply worsted made of Norwegian wool. Heilo Yarns are now available in the United States and may be obtained from the sources listed at the end of this Introduction.

If you are unable to procure Heilo Yarn, another good quality four-ply sports worsted may be substituted. It is important that dyes be fast so that they will not run in the wash.

Norwegian garments are designed to be wind and waterproof, being very tightly knit on #0, #1 or #2 needles, at the gauge or tension specified at the beginning of each pattern. It is a combination of yarn, needles and the knitting style of the individual that determines gauge. Tight knitters may need larger needles to achieve the proper tension whereas loose knitters can attain it with smaller needles. The only way to find out what size needles you need in order to achieve the indicated tension is to experiment: cast on the number of stitches listed in the "Tension" section of the pattern you are planning to use; work in the pattern indicated for the number of rows specified; cast the piece off and steam it gently to block it. Then measure the piece carefully. If you have too many stitches or rows to the inch, try to knit looser or use a larger needle; if you have too few stitches or rows, try knitting tighter or use a smaller needle. Experiment until you get it right. Don't try to avoid the problem by casting on more or fewer stitches than specified, for you will soon find yourself involved in higher mathematics while trying to make the complex patterns "come out right."

Special attention is drawn to the fact that Norwegian sweaters are made larger than most other sweaters in order to insure comfort and warmth. The usual practice is to allow at least an extra two inches in girth in order to enable the wearer to move freely when skiing and to allow an insulating air-current to circulate between the body and the knitwear. Norwegian sweaters and jackets are also longer than other garments in order to protect the lower back when one is exposed to the cold winter weather.

Since this book was originally intended for use by the British knitter, several British terms are used: i.e., the word "jumper" is used for a pullover, and what most Americans would call a "cardigan" is here referred to as a "jacket." Although American sizes of knitting needles are indicated in the list of materials at the beginning of each pattern, needle sizes are referred to by their British counterparts in the text. Note that the British #13 needle equals the American #0, and the British #10 equals the American #3. The yarn balls listed under "Materials" are of the standard 50-gram type.

SOME HINTS ON PATTERN OR "FAIR ISLE" KNITTING

The technical name for knitting attractive designs in several colors is "Fair Isle" knitting. All of the patterns in this book are drawn on grids in which each square equals one stitch. In the sample pattern (Figure 1), the white squares represent one color and the crossed squares another color. From A to B there are eight stitches. After B the same pattern repeats through the row, and the total number of stitches must therefore be divisible by eight.

If you prefer knitting on two needles, the method is as follows: take two balls of wool of different colors, but of the same thickness and cast on the required number of stitches. We shall call the colors here black and white.

1st row: (A to B) 2 white stitches, 1 black, 1 white, 1 black, 2 white, 1 black.
2nd row: (B to A) 2 black stitches, 2 white, 1 black, 2 white, 1 black.
3rd row: (A to B) 2 black stitches, 3 white, 2 black, 1 white.
4th row: (B to A) 2 white stitches, 2 black, 1 white, 2 black, 1 white.

In Norway, knitting is often done on circular needles, and detailed instructions for knitting with circular needles are given later on in this Introduction. If you want to knit round in pattern instead of to and fro, the method is as follows: cast an entire row of stitches onto a circular needle or onto a set of double-pointed needles forming a square:

1st round: 2 white stitches, 1 black, 1 white, 1 black, 2 white, 1 black, etc.
2nd round: 1 black stitch, 2 white, 1 black, 2 white, etc.
3rd round: 2 black stitches, 3 white, 2 black, 1 white, etc.
4th round: 1 white stitch, 2 black, 1 white, 2 black, 3 white, etc.

In Fair Isle knitting there are two methods of carrying the yarn across the wrong side of the work. Many knitters use "weaving in," a method by which the colored thread not being knitted is woven into every other stitch. Norwegian garments are traditionally knit by the method known as "stranding," in which the unused wool is carried loosely across the back of the work to give a beautiful even finish to the garment. In this method both colors are held at the back of the work. The top diagram in Figure 2 shows the method of knitting with the right hand (light stitches) while "stranding" with the left. The right hand is shown about to make the next stitch as indicated by the arrow while the left hand is shown holding the dark wool along the back of the work. As long as the light stitches are being knit this action is repeated; the left hand keeping the dark wool below and out of the way of the light wool. One must be careful to keep the stranding wool at an even tension.

The lower diagram in Figure 2 shows the dark

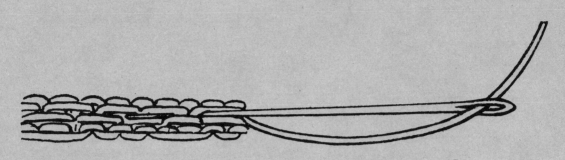

Figure 3

color in use and the light color being stranded across. The arrow indicates the movement of the needle for the first dark-colored stitch.

Whatever method is used, Fair Isle knitting should have the same elasticity as ordinary stocking stitch. Do not draw the wool too tightly; keep the work reasonably loose on the reverse side, or the pattern will not emerge properly.

Wools can be joined by knitting 2-3 stitches with double wool (namely the end of the old with the beginning of the new). Then, using a thick darning needle, all loose ends are darned in horizontally on the wrong side, preferably through the back of the same colored stitches. (See Figure 3.)

SOME HINTS ON MAKING NORWEGIAN SWEATERS WITH A CIRCULAR NEEDLE

All of the garments in this book can be knit on two needles, but in Norway circular needles are used to knit Fair Isle sweaters and jackets. This method is both simple and practical. The entire body of the garment is knit in one piece, eliminating side seams, armhole and shoulder shapings, and the difficulty in matching patterns.

Figure 4 shows all of the stitches placed on a circular needle. With the right side facing, one continues knitting round and round in plain knitting, thus avoiding turning and purling on the wrong side. When the required length to the shoulder is obtained, all of the stitches are cast off.

The design is worked according to the appropriate diagram. The patterns in this book are com-

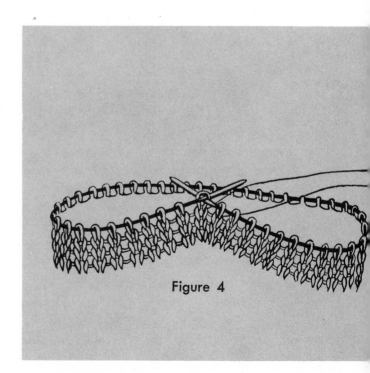

Figure 4

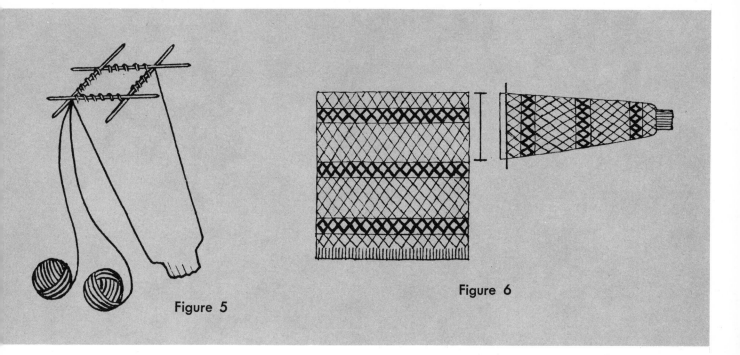

Figure 5

Figure 6

piled so that rounds begin and end with a complete motif, but it is a good idea to place a marker where the round begins.

Sleeves are knit in the same way on double-pointed sock needles, thus also avoiding any seams. The shape is obtained by increasing on the underarm. When the required width is obtained, all the stitches are cast off. Figure 5 shows the sleeve on four needles. In the United States, usually only three needles are used.

PREPARING THE GARMENT

The body of the garment is knit to the required length to the shoulder, and then all stitches are cast off. Sleeves are knit according to the usual length of the underarm seam and end with 4 rows of plain color for a seam. Cast off loosely. Using a warm iron, press all pieces under a damp cloth. Do not press the ribbing as this destroys the elasticity. Pin cast-off edges to the ironing cloth as they have a tendency to curl when damp. Gently smooth into shape, but do not brush or rub. (See Figure 6.)

CUTTING THE ARMHOLE

Always keep the right side of the work facing you when making up the garment. Now arrange the armhole by placing the garment flat on a table with the beginning of the rounds (where the pattern may be slightly irregular) at one side for a pullover, or at the center front for a cardigan. Before cutting the armholes, check to make sure that the pattern on what will be the front and back of the sweater is exactly the same. Measure the width

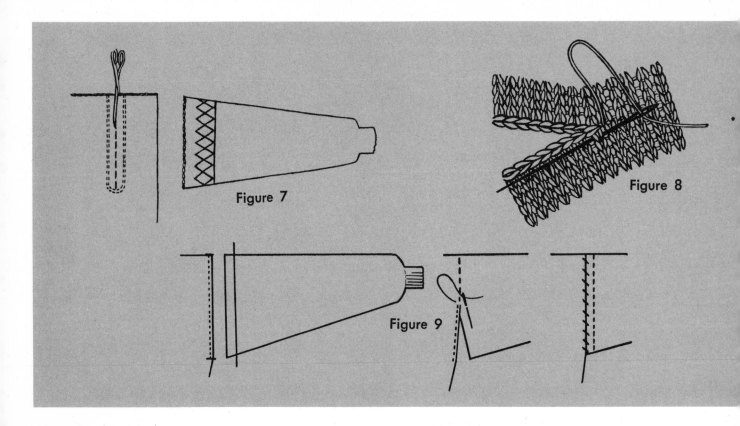

Figure 7

Figure 8

Figure 9

of the sleeve tops and mark that measurement on the garment proper for armholes. Place a row of basting threads where the armhole will come. Make a row of machine stitching on each side of the basting stitches, being especially careful to keep the sewing machine tension fairly loose in order not to stretch the knitted fabric. Cut along the basting stitches between the two rows of machine stitching. It is no more difficult to cut knitwear than any other fabric, and the machine stitching prevents fraying. (See Figure 7.)

In most of the patterns in this book, the armhole comes *below* the shoulder. Experience has proven that this kimono-style armhole is the most comfortable for sportswear and well-suited to the thicker-ply wool used in this type of Norwegian knitwear.

JOINING THE SHOULDERS

It is easy to match patterns by joining the shoulder seams by hand on the right side.

With the right side of the work facing you, carefully join front and back shoulders in the left hand. Using a thick darning needle and a suitable wool thread (preferably matching the darkest color in the pattern), sew from right to left in this manner:

hold the needle parallel to the cast-off edge and sew under a stitch just beyond the cast-off edge, then under a stitch on the opposite shoulder. (See Figure 8.) Continue in this manner throughout. When the wool is tightened, the cast-off edges will be drawn on to the wrong side, leaving a machine-like seam.

One can also machine stitch, backstitch, overcast or crochet the shoulders together through the cast-off edges on the wrong side.

If the sweater has a straight neckline, in line with the shoulder (as shown in Figure 6), end the work by knitting one purl round and 5 rounds stocking stitch for a facing before casting off. Fold on the purl round and hem the facing on the wrong side. Then, using double wool join the shoulders on the right side by overcasting through each purl loop, leaving a large enough opening in the center for the head.

ATTACHING THE SLEEVES

With the right side of the work facing you, place the last 4 (facing) rounds of the sleeve inside the armhole, and pin into position, matching centers to shoulder seams. Using a thick darning needle

X

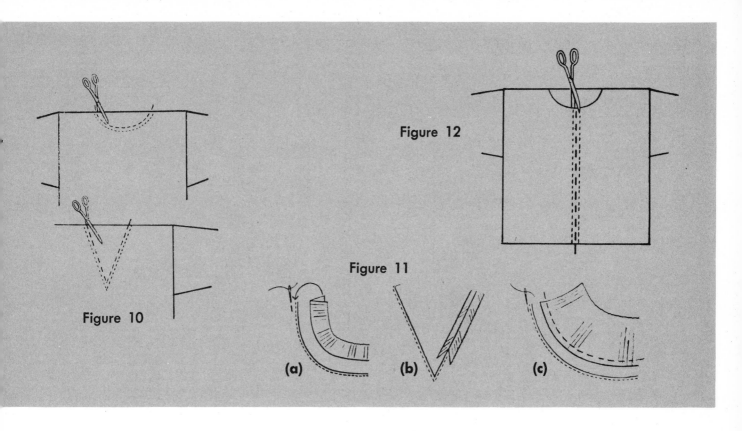

Figure 12

Figure 11

Figure 10

(a) (b) (c)

and suitably colored wool, hold the needle parallel to the armhole and sew in the first stitch beyond the machine stitching around the armhole (folding cut edge to wrong side). Then sew in one stitch in the fifth round of the sleeve. Continue sewing alternately in the garment and the sleeve along a chain of stitches, thus ensuring a straight seam. Having attached sleeves, hem around the armhole facings to make a neat edge. (See Figure 9.)

MAKING THE NECKLINE

Mark on the sweater the type of neckline preferred, either round or V-necked. The same basic method is used for both necklines. Outline the chosen shape with a row of basting thread and sew two rows of machine stitches just below the basting. Again, adjust the tension on the sewing machine so that the knitted fabric will not pull. Remove the surplus knitted material by cutting on the basting line. (See Figure 10.)

There are two methods for making a neckband. In the first method (Figure 11a) a straight piece of ribbing twice as wide as the desired band width is knit either on two needles or on a circular needle. The piece is then attached to the neckline, doubled over and attached to the wrong side for a facing, and hemmed around to cover raw edges. If knitted on a circular needle there will be no seam. If knitted on two needles, the resulting seam should be placed in line with the left shoulder seam. For a V-neck (Figure 11b) one gradually decreases, then increases until the required shape is obtained.

In the second method a single-width neckband is knit. (See Figure 11c.) In this case, the last 4 rows are placed inside the neckline in the same manner as sleeves are attached (Figure 9) and hemmed around to cover the raw edges.

SPECIAL INSTRUCTIONS FOR JACKETS AND CARDIGANS

Cutting out the neckline of a jacket or cardigan is done in much the same manner as cutting out the neckline of a pullover. (See Figure 10.)

To make the front opening, place a basting thread in the center front chain of stitches. Sew a row of machine stitching along each side of the basting thread, and then cut along the basting thread. (See Figure 12.)

For a jacket with a round neck, knit a border of knit-one purl-one ribbing which, when slightly

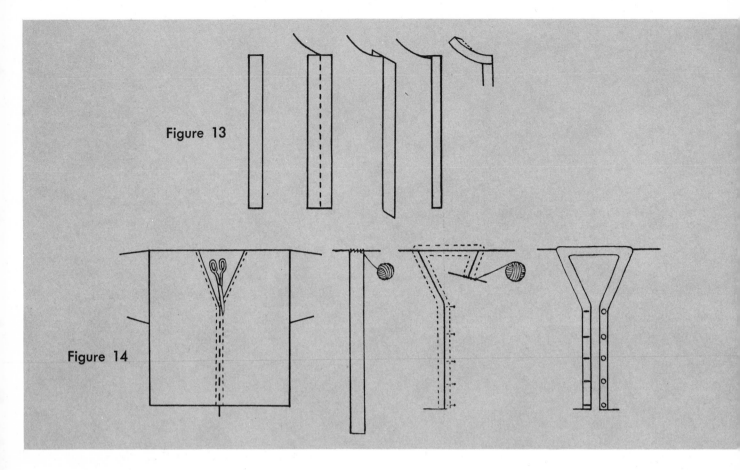

Figure 13

Figure 14

stretched, will reach from hem to neckline. Knit the border for the button side first. Pin the border onto the jacket so that the facing protrudes beyond the cut edge. (See Figure 13.) Using a matching thread, machine stitch along the border just beyond the machine stitching on the jacket. Fold the facing to the wrong side, thus covering the cut edge, and hem down. The border can also be attached by hand, using a matching wool and sewing one stitch in the jacket and one in the border, as was done to attach sleeves. (See Figure 9.) Mark positions of the buttons and knit another border with buttonholes to correspond.

The neckband is knit double and attached from the right side, folded at the center and hemmed around on the wrong side. (See Figure 11a.) If a buttonhole is required in the neckband, a corresponding one must be made in the facing so that they will fit together as one.

For a jacket with a V-neck, the borders and neckband are all knit in one piece. (See Figure 14.) Pin the button side into position, mark for buttons; continue around the neck, and complete, making buttonholes to correspond to the buttons. Attach as explained above.

Press borders before attaching buttons. Pewter buttons are traditional on Norwegian cardigans.

For additional information on knitting with circular needles, follow the more detailed instructions pertaining to the specific garment you wish to make.

SOURCES OF SUPPLY

Heilo Yarn may be obtained from the following sources:

Gagga's Import, 22 A Avenue, Lake Oswego, Oregon 97034

The Wichelt, Rural Route 1, Stoddard, Wisc. 54658

S. & S. Import, 5123 Cribari Place, San Jose, Calif. 95135

Scandinavian Design, Box 1353, Aspen, Colo. 81611

Old Sautee Store, Sautee Nacoochee, Georgia 30571

Vanberia Scandinavian Imports, Mrs. Hamlet Petersen, 217 West Water Street, Decorah, Iowa 52101

The Green Door Needlecraft Shop, Boulder, Colo. 80302

KNIT
YOUR OWN

NORWEGIAN
SWEATERS

SHOWN IN COLOR ON FRONT COVER.

LADY'S JUMPER AND CAP

Size to fit 32—34—36—38 inch bust

Materials:

Size	32/34	36	38	
	8	9	10	balls White no. 501.
	7	8	9	« Red no. 813 or Green no. 733 or Yellow no. 787.
	2	3	3	« Red no. 821 or Green no. 734 or Mustard no. 748.

A pair of needles each no. 10 and 13 or 2 circular needles and set of needles each no. 10 and 13.

Actual measurements:

Size	32	34	36	38		
All round	36	37½	40	41½	ins. approx.	
Length	24	25	26	27	«	«
Sleeve seam	19	19	20	20	«	«

American	14	16	18	20		SIZE OF NEEDLES	0	3
British							13	10

TENSION:

26 stitches and 30 rows in pattern on no. 10 needles = 4 inches.
Check your tension very carefully. Adjust by using thicker or thinner needles.

ABBREVIATIONS:

Beg., beginning; cont., continue; fin., finishing; inc., increase; inc. 1 st., pick up loop between sts. and k. into back of same; k., knit; patt., pattern; p., purl; rem., remaining; rep., repeat; rd., round; sts., stitches; st.st., stocking stitch; tog., together; G., Green; Mc., Main colour; M., Mustard; R., Red.

TWO NEEDLE METHOD

BACK AND FRONT ALIKE:

Using no. 13 needles and Mc. cast on 121—127—133—139 sts. and work 1½ ins. in k.1, p.1 rib, fin. on wrong side.

Change to st.st. (k. on right, p. on wrong side). Work 2 rows, change to no. 10 needles. x. Cont. in patt. from chart, beg. as indicated. Complete borders I, II and III. Then cont. as follows:

Size 32: Using Mc. k.1 row, k.1 row on wrong side to form a stripe, work 5 rows st.st. for facing. Cast off.

Size 34: Using R. no. 698 or G. no. 734 or M. 683 work 8 rows, p.1 row on right side to form a stripe, work 5 rows st.st. for facing. Cast off.

Size 36: Work 8 rows as for size 34, cont. in Mc. work 8 rows more, p.1 row on right side to form a stripe, work 5 rows st.st. for facing. Cast off.

Size 38: As for size 36 but work 1½ ins. in Mc. Cast off.

SLEEVES:

Two sets of figures only, denote the first and last two sizes. Using no. 13 needles and Mc. cast on 60—66 sts. and work as Back to x. Inc. 1 st. at beg. of last row. Then inc. 1 st. within the first and last st. every 8th row until there are 101—109 sts. Cont. in patt. as follows: Complete the last 22—28 rows of border I, entire border II, the first 52 rows of border III. Then complete border III, inc. likewise on every row. 127—135 sts. Finally p.1 row on right side to form a stripe, p.1 row on wrong side. Cast off.

TO MAKE UP:

Darn in all loose ends. Omitting ribbing press work on wrong side with a hot iron over a damp cloth. Allow to dry. Join shoulders sewing through the p. stripe. Leave 9 ins. open for neck. Slip st. around facing. Join sides and sleeves, edge to edge flat seams. Attach sleeves carefully matching centres to shoulders. Sew through the p. stripe and in second chain of sts. on Jumper. Press all seams.

CAP:

Using no. 13. needles and Mc. cast on 126 sts., all sizes, and work 1 inch in k.1, p.1 rib, fin. on wrong side. Inc. 1 st. at beg. of last row. Change to no. 10 needles and st.st. Complete the first 54 rows of border I. K.2 sts. tog. at end of last row. Next row: K.6, k.2 tog. x K.12, k.2 tog. x. Rep. from x—x, 7 times, k.6 sts. Cont. with 1 st. less at beg. or end also between each shaping on every row until 18 sts. rem. Thread double wool through same. Press. Join and press seam. Draw together at top and fasten well. Twist or crochet an 8-inch cord using 8 lengths of wool. Make a tassel and attach to end of same. Attach the other end to crown.

CIRCULAR KNITTING METHOD

BODY OF JUMPER:

Using circular needle no. 13 and Mc. cast on 240—252—264—276 sts. and work 1½ ins. in k.1, p.1 rib. Change to st.st. (k. all rds.) K.1 rd. then change to circular needle no. 10. Cont. in patt. from chart, beg. as indicated. Complete borders I, II and III. Cont. as follows:

Size 32: Using Mc. k.1 rd., p.1 rd., k.5 rds. for facing. Cast off.

Size 34: Using R. no. 698 or G. no. 734 or M. no. 683 k.8 rds., p.1 rd., k.5 rds. for facing. Cast off.

Size 36: K.8 rds. as for size 34. Cont. in Mc. k.8 rds. more, p.1 rd., k.5 rds. for facing. Cast off.

Size 38: As for size 36 but k.1½ ins. in Mc. Cast off.

SLEEVES:

Two sets of figures only, denote the first and last two sizes. Using set of needles no. 13 and Mc. cast on 60—66 sts. and

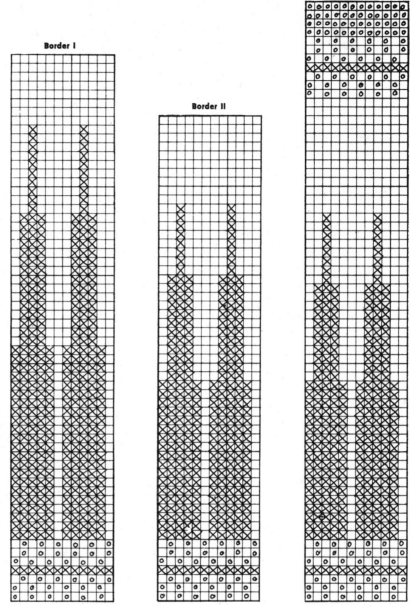

Border I

Border II

Border III

☐ = White

✗ = Red or Green or Yellow

o = Red or Green or Mustard

work as for Jumper as far as x. Inc. 1 st. at beg. of rd. Then inc. 2 sts. at underarm, 1 st. at either side of the first and last st. every 8th rd. until there are 101—109 sts. Cont. in patt. as follows: Complete the last 22—28 rds. of border I, entire border II and the first 52 rds. of border III. Then complete border III, inc. likewise on every rd. 127—135 sts. Finally turn work inside out and k.6 rds. for seam facing. Cast off.

TO MAKE UP:

Darn in all loose ends. Press. Measure width of sleeve tops and mark corresponding length on Jumper for armholes. Make sure that patts. match at armholes. Machine twice around armholes, to prevent fraying and cut between the machining. Join shoulders sewing through the p. stripe on right side of work. Leave 9 ins. open for neck. Slip st. around facing. Attach

sleeves carefully matching centres to shoulders. Sew through the first p. rd. and in chain of sts. just beyond the machining around armholes. Press seam, fold facing over raw edges on wrong side and slip st. to neaten. Press well.

CAP:

Using set of needles no. 13 and Mc. cast on 126 sts., all sizes, and work 1 inch in k.1, p.1 rib. Change to st.st. K.1 rd., inc. 1 st. at beg. of same. Change to set of needles no. 10. Complete the first 54 rds. of border I. K.2 sts. tog. at end of last rd. Next rd.: K.6, k.2 tog. x K.12, k.2 tog. x. Rep. from x—x, 7 times, k.6 sts. Cont. with 1 st. less at beg. or end also between each shaping on every rd. until 18 sts. rem. Thread double wool through same. Press. Draw together at top and fasten well. Complete as for two needle method.

SHOWN IN COLOR ON PAGE 28.

LADY'S JUMPER, AND CHILD'S JUMPER AND CAP

Size to fit 32-34-36-37 inch bust, 4-6-8-10 years.

Materials:

Size 32/34	36/37			4	6	8	10		
10	11	balls White no. 501.		7	8	9	10	balls Blue no. 707.
4	4	« Light blue no. 608.		2	3	3	4	« White no. 501.

A pair of needles each no. 10 and 13 or 2 circular needles and set of needles each no. 10 and 13.

American		SIZE OF NEEDLES	0	3
British			13	10

TENSION:

26 stitches and 32 rows in main pattern on no. 10 needles = 4 inches.

Check your tension very carefully. Adjust by using thicker or thinner needles.

ABBREVIATIONS:

Beg., beginning; cont., continue; fin., finishing; inc., increase; inc. 1 st., pick up loop between sts. and k. into back of same; k., knit; patt., pattern; p., purl; rem., remaining; rd., round; sts., stitches; st. st. stocking stitch; Mc., Main colour.

TWO NEEDLE METHOD

Two sets of figures only, denote the first and last two sizes. Child's sizes are in parentheses.

BACK AND FRONT ALIKE:

Using no. 13 needles and Mc. cast on 120—130 (90—100—100—110) sts. and work 1½ ins. in k. 1, p. 1 rib, fin. on wrong side. Change to no. 10 needles and st. st., k. on right, p. on wrong side. K. 1 row, inc. 1 st. at end of same.

Cont. in patt. from chart, beg. as indicated. Complete border I, cont. in main patt. until entire work measures 15½—16—16½—17½ (8½—10—11—12) ins. Then shape armholes: Cast off 3 sts. at beg. of next 2 rows, dec. 1 st. likewise twice until 111—121 (81—91—91—101) sts. rem. Cont. in main patt. until entire work measures 22—23—23½—24 (13—14½—16—17½) ins., fin. with 3 patt. rows. Complete border II. Finally p. 1 row on right side to form a stripe, work 5 rows st. st. for facing. Cast off.

4

SLEEVES:

Using no. 13 needles and Mc. cast on 60 (50) sts., all sizes. Work as Jumper as far as border I. Having completed same cont. in main patt. Inc. 1 st. within the first and last st. every 8th row until there are 97—99—99—101 (73—75—77—81) sts. When entire sleeve measures 16½—17—17½—18 (10—11½—12—13½) ins., fin. with 3 patt. rows, complete border II. Inc. likewise every 2nd row thrice (4th row twice) then on the last 12 (8) rows until there are 127—129—129—131 (93—95—97—101) sts. Finally p. 2 rows to form a stripe on right side. Cast off.

TO MAKE UP:

Darn in all loose ends. Omitting ribbing press work on wrong side with a hot iron over a damp cloth. Allow to dry. Join shoulders sewing through the p. stripe on right side. Leave 9(7—8) ins. open for neck. Slip st. around facing. Join sides and sleeves, edge to edge flat seams. Attach sleeves carefully matching centres to shoulders. Sew through the p. stripe and in second chain of sts. on Jumper. Press all seams.

CAP:

Using no. 13 needles and Mc. cast on 120—130 sts. and work 1½ ins. in k. 1, p. 1 rib, fin. on wrong side. Change to no. 10 needles and st. st. K. 1 row, inc. 1 st. at end of same. Complete border II, upside down, cont. in main patt. until entire work measures 8—8—8½—9½ ins.
Next row: K. 2 sts. together throughout. K. 1 row. Thread double wool through rem. sts.

TO MAKE UP:

Press. Join and press seam. Draw together at top and fasten well. Make a large pompon using both colours and attach to crown.

CIRCULAR KNITTING METHOD

BODY OF JUMPER:

Using circular needle no. 13 and Mc. cast on 240—260 (180—200—200—220) sts. and work 1½ ins. in k. 1, p. 1 rib. K. 1 rd., change to circular needle no. 10. Cont. in st. st., k. all rds., and patt. from chart, beg. as indicated. Complete border I, cont. in main patt. until entire work measures 22—23—23½—24 (13—14½—16—17½) ins. fin. with 3 patt. rds. Complete border II. Finally p. 1 rd., k. 5 rds. for facing. Cast off.

SLEEVES:

Using set of needles no. 13 and Mc. cast on 60 (50) sts., all sizes. Work the welt as before. K. 1 rd., inc. 1 st. at end of same. Change to set of needles no. 10. Complete border I. Cont. in main patt., inc. 2 sts. at underarm, 1 st. within the first and last st. every 8th rd. until there are 97—99—99—101 (73—75—77—81) sts. When entire sleeve measures 16½—17—17½—18 (10—11½—12—13½) ins., fin. with 3 patt. rds., complete border II. Inc. likewise every 2nd rd. thrice (4th rd. twice) then on the last 12 (8) rds. until there are 127—129—129—131 (93—95—97—101) sts. Finally turn work inside out and k. 6 rds. for facing. Cast off.

TO MAKE UP:

Darn in all loose ends. Press. Measure width of sleeve tops and mark corresponding length on Jumper for armholes. Make sure that patts. match at armholes. Machine twice around armholes, to prevent fraying, in chain of sts. and cut between the machining.

Join shoulders sewing through the p. stripe on right side. Leave 9 (7—8) ins. open for neck. Slip st. around facing. Attach sleeves carefully matching centres to shoulders. Sew through the p. stripe and in chain of sts. just beyond the machining around armholes. Press seam. Fold facing over raw edges on wrong side and slip st. to neaten. Press well.

CAP:

Using set of needles no. 13 and Mc. cast on 120—130 sts. and work 1½ ins. in k. 1, p. 1 rib. Change to set of needles no. 10 and st. st. K. 1 rd. Complete border II, upside down. Cont. in main patt. until entire work measures 8—8—8½—9½ ins. Complete as for Two Needle Method.

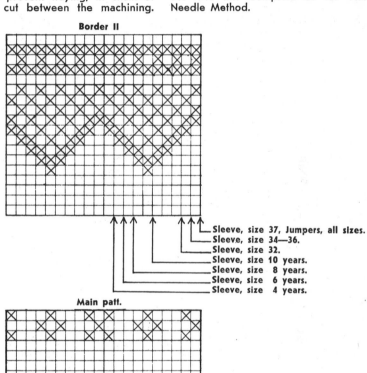

Border II

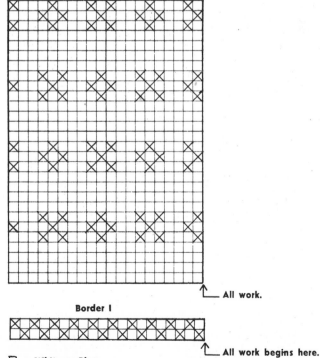

Sleeve, size 37, Jumpers, all sizes.
Sleeve, size 34—36.
Sleeve, size 32.
Sleeve, size 10 years.
Sleeve, size 8 years.
Sleeve, size 6 years.
Sleeve, size 4 years.

Main patt.

All work.

Border I

All work begins here.

□ = White or Blue.
X = Light blue or White.

SHOWN IN COLOR ON PAGE 26.

LADY'S JUMPER AND MAN'S JACKET

Size to fit 32-34-36-37 inch bust, 38-40-41-44 inch chest.

Materials:

Size 32/34	36/37			38	40/41	44	
9	10	balls White no. 501.		12	13	14	balls Marine no. 584.
5	6	« Light blue no. 707.		6	7	8	« White no. 501.
2	3	« Marine no. 584.		3	3	3	« Red no. 681.

A pair of needles each no. 10 and 13 or 2 circular needles and set of needles each no. 10 and 13. 6 pewter buttons for Jacket.

American	SIZE OF NEEDLES	0	3
British		13	10

TENSION:
26 stitches and 30 rows in pattern on no. 10 needles = 4 inches.
Check your tension very carefully. Adjust by using thicker or thinner needles.

ABBREVIATIONS:
Beg., beginning; cont., continue; fin., finishing; inc., increase; inc. 1 st., pick up loop between sts. and k. into back of same; k., knit; patt., pattern; p., purl; rem., remaining; rep., repeat; rd., round; sts., stitches; st. st., stocking stitch; M., Marine.

TWO NEEDLE METHOD
LADIES JUMPER:
BACK AND FRONT ALIKE:
Two sets of figures only, denote the first and last two sizes.

Using no. 13 needles and M. cast on 120—130 sts. and work 1½ ins. in k. 1, p. 1 rib, fin. on wrong side. Change to st. st. (k. on right, p. on wrong side.) Work 2 rows, inc. 1 st. at beg. of last row. Change to no. 10 needles. x. Cont. in patt. from chart. Complete borders I, II twice, III, IV. Rep. in the same sequence but work border II once. For size 36 and 37 work the last 9 rows of border IV. Finally, all sizes, cont. in M., p. 1 row on right side, work 5 rows st. st. for facing. Cast off.

SLEEVES:
Using no. 13 needles and M. cast on 60 sts., all sizes. Work 1½—2 ins. in rib as before. Work as Back at far as x. Cont. in patt. Inc. 1 st. within the first and last st. every 8th row until there are 101 sts. Complete border I, last 20 rows of border II, last 10 rows of border III, last 32 rows of border IV. Rep. in same sequence fin. with border IV, omitting the last 7 rows. Complete borders IV and I, inc. likewise on each of these 12 rows. 125 sts. Finally p. 1 row on right side, k. 1 row on wrong side. Cast off.

TO MAKE UP:
Darn in all loose ends. Omitting ribbing press work on wrong side with a hot iron over a damp cloth. Join shoulders sewing through the p. stripe on right side. Leave 9 ins. open for neck. Slip st. around facing. Join sides and sleeves, edge to edge flat seams. Attach sleeves carefully matching centres to shoulders. Sew through the p. stripe and in second chain of sts. on Jumper. Press all seams.

MAN'S JACKET:
BACK:
Using no. 13 needles and M. cast on 130—140—140—150 sts. and work 1½ ins. in rib, fin on wrong side. Change to st. st. and work 2 rows, inc. 1 st. at beg. of last row. Change to no. 10 needles. Cont. in patt. from chart. x. Complete borders I, II twice, III, IV. Rep. in the same sequence, rep. border I again. Then work each shoulder separately. Allow 45—48—48—52 sts. for each. P. 1 row on right side, work 5 rows st. st. for facing. Cast off. Cast off rem. sts. for neck.

RIGHT FRONT:
Using no. 13 needles and M. cast on 77—82—82—87 sts. and work welt as before, fin. on right side. Change to st. st., beg. on a p. row. P. 65—70—70—75 sts., inc. 1 st. for seam, (to be worked in plain colour throughout), leave rem. 12 sts. on a holder for Front Band. K. 1 row, inc. 1 st. at end of same. Change to no. 10 neeedles. Cont. in patt. to match Back. On 28th row of second border IV shape for neck: Beg. on k. row cast off the seam st. then the next 5—6—6—7 sts. P. back. Next row: Cast off 4—5—5—5 sts. then dec. at beg. of k. rows 3 sts. twice, 2 sts. twice, 1 st. twice until 45—48—48—52 sts. rem. for shoulder. Finally using M., p. 1 row on right side, work 5 rows st. st. for facing. Cast off.

LEFT FRONT:
Work as Right Front for 1 inch, fin. on wrong side. Next row: Rib to last 9 sts., cast off 5 sts. for buttonhole, rib to end. On next row cast on 5 sts. over those cast off. Cont. until welt measures 1½ ins., fin. on wrong side. Change to st. st. K. 65—70—70—75 sts., inc. 1 st. (to be worked in plain colour throughout), leave rem. 12 sts. on a holder. P. 1 row, inc. 1 st. at end of same. Change to no. 10 needles. Cont. to match Right Front. Shape neck at beg. of p. rows.

SLEEVES:
Using no. 13 needles and M. cast on 70 sts., all sizes. Work as Back as far as x. Inc. 1 st. within the first and last st. every 8th row until there are 117 sts. Complete borders I to IV twice. Inc. likewise on each of the last 14 rows of second border IV. 145 sts. Finally using M., p. 1 row on right side, k. 1 row on wrong side. Cast off.

BUTTON BAND:

Using no. 13 needles and M. pick up the sts. from Right Front, inc. 1 st. at inner edge for seam. Cont. in rib until band, when slightly stretched, reaches neckline. Then cast off the seam st., leave rem. sts. on a holder. Attach to Front Mark position of buttons, spacing evenly. Allow for one in neckband. (6 in all).

BUTTONHOLE BAND:

Work to match making corresponding buttonholes as before.

TO MAKE UP:

Join shoulders. Otherwise as for Jumper.

NECKBAND:

Using no. 13 needles and M. pick up the 12 sts. from Right Front, 115—119 —119—121 sts. around neck, 12 sts. from Left Front. Work 2½ ins. in rib as before. Make a buttonhole after ½ inch and again after 1½ ins. Cast off loosely. Fold in half on to wrong side and slip st. Sew around buttonholes. Attach buttons.

☐ = White or Marine.
✕ = Light blue or White.
○ = Marine or Red.

Border I

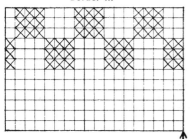

Border II

Border III

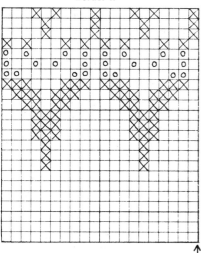

Border IV

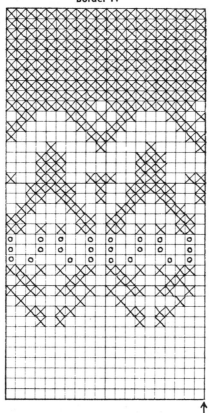

All work and sizes begin as indicated.

CIRCULAR KNITTING METHOD

LADY'S JUMPER:

Using circular needle no. 13 and M. cast on 240—260 sts. and work 1½ ins. in k. 1, p. 1 rib. Change to st. st. (k. all rds.) K. 1 rd. Change to circular needle no. 10. Cont. in patt., from chart. Work the borders in same sequence as for Two Needle Method. Finally using M., p. 1 rd., k. 5 rds. for facing. Cast off.

SLEEVES:

Using set of needles no. 13 and M. cast on 60 sts., all sizes. Work 1½—2 ins. in rib as before. Work as Jumper as far as x. Cont. in patt. in same border sequence as for Two Needle Method. Inc. 2 sts. at underarm, 1 st. at either side of the first and last st. every 8th rd. until there are 101 sts. Further inc. as for Two Needle Method. 125 sts. Finally turn the sleeve inside out and k. 6 rds. in M. for seam facing. Cast off.

TO MAKE UP:

Darn in all loose ends. Press. Measure width of sleeve tops and mark corresponding length on Jumper for armholes. Make sure patts. match at armholes. Machine twice around armholes, to prevent fraying, in chain of sts. and cut between the machining. Join shoulders sewing through the p. stripe on right side. Leave 9 ins. open for neck. Slip st. around facing. Attach sleeves carefully matching centres to shoulders. Sew through the p. stripe and in chain

of sts. just beyond the machining around armholes. Press seam. Fold facing over raw edges on wrong side and slip st. to neaten. Press well.

MAN'S JACKET:

Using circular needle no. 13 and M. cast on 285—305—305—325 sts. and work in k. 1, p. 1 rib for 1 inch, to and fro, fin. on wrong side.
Next row: Rib to within last 9 sts., cast off 5 sts. for buttonhole, rib to end. On next row cast on 5 sts. over those cast off. Cont. in rib until welt measures 1½ ins.
Next row: Rib 12 sts., place on a holder, k. to last 12 sts., place on a holder for Front Band. Change to circular needle no. 10. Cast on 3 sts. and join work into a rd. Work these sts. in plain colour. The work is cut here later. 264 —284—284—304 sts. Cont. in patt. sequence as for Two Needle Method. On 27th rd. of second border IV shape neck. Cast off the last 5—6—6—7 sts. also the centre 3 sts. On next rd. cast off the first 5—6—6—7 sts., k. to end of rd. From here work to and fro, p. on wrong side. Cast off at beg. of every row 3—4—4—4 sts. then 3 sts. twice, 2 sts. twice, 1 st. twice until 221—237— 237—255 sts. rem. Cont. in M. and k. 1 row. Then work each shoulder separately. Allow 45—48—48—52 sts. for each. Finally p. 1 row on right side, k. 5 rows for facing. Cast off. Cast off rem. sts. for neck.

SLEEVES:

Using set of needles no. 13 and M. cast on 70 sts., all sizes. Work 2 ins. in rib as before. Change to st. st. K. 1 rd., inc. 1 st. at end of same. Cont. in patt. Inc. 2 sts. at underarm, 1 st. within the first and last st. every 8th rd., working the extra sts. into patt., until there are 117 sts. Work in same patt sequence and inc. likewise as for Two Needle Method. Finally turn sleeve inside out and k. 6 rds. for seam facing. Cast off.

BUTTON BAND:

Using no. 13 needles and M. cast on 5 sts. for facing then pick up the 12 sts., from Right Front. Cont. in rib but work the facing in st. st. until band, when slightly stretched, reaches neckline. Then cast off the 5 sts. and leave rem. sts. on a holder. Mark position of buttons, spacing evenly, allow for one in neckband. (6 in all.)

BUTTONHOLE BAND:

Work to match making corresponding buttonholes as before.

TO MAKE UP:

Darn in all loose ends. Press. Join shoulders. Otherwise as for Lady's Jumper. Machine twice along centre front and cut between the machining. Attach Front Bands. Press seam, fold facing over raw edges on wrong side and slip st.

NECKBAND:

As for Two Needle Method.

SHOWN IN COLOR ON PAGE 28.

MAN'S SWEATER AND LADY'S JACKET

Size to fit 38-40-42-43 inch chest, 34-35-37-38 inch bust.

Materials:

Size 38/40	42/43			34/35	37/38		
12	13	balls	Charcoal no. 12.	11	12	balls	White no. 501 or 17.
5	6	«	White no. 501.	5	6	«	Dark green no. 734.
3	4	«	Grey no. 5.	3	3	«	Light green no. 733.

A pair of needles each no. 10 and 13 or 2 circular needles an set of needles each no. 10 and 13.

American		SIZE OF NEEDLES	0	3
British			13	10

8

TENSION:

26 stitches and 30 rows in pattern on no. 10 needles = 4 inches.
Check your tension very carefully. Adjust by using thicker or thinner needles.

ABBREVIATIONS:

Beg., beginning; cont., continue; dec., decrease; fin., finishing; inc., increase; inc 1 st., pick up loop between sts. and k. into back of same; k., knit; patt., pattern; p., purl; rem., remaining; rep., repeat; rd., round; sts., stitches; st.st., stocking stitch; C., Charcoal; Dg., Dark green.

TWO NEEDLE METHOD

MENS SWEATER:

Two sets of figures only, denote the first and last two sizes.

BACK AND FRONT ALIKE:

Using no. 13 needles and C. cast on 140—150 sts. and work 1½ ins. in k. 1, p. 1 rib, fin. on wrong side. Change to st.st. (k. on right, p. on wrong side). Work 2 rows, inc. 1 st. at beg. of last row then change to no. 10 needles. Cont. in patt. from chart. beg. as indicated. x Complete borders I, II, III, II, III, II. Cont. as follows:
Size 38/40: Using C. work 4 rows then border I.
Size 42/43: Complete the first 15 rows of border III then border I.
All sizes: Using C. k. 2 rows to form a p. stripe on right side, work 5 rows st.st. for facing. Cast off.

SLEEVES:

Using no. 13 needles and C. cast on 70 sts., all sizes and work as for Back to x. In 1 st. within the first and last st. every 8th row, working the extra sts. into patt., until there are 113—115 sts. Complete borders I, II, III, II then cont. as follows:
Size 38/40: Complete the first 32 rows of border III, inc. likewise on each of the last 10 rows. 133 sts. Complete border I, inc. likewise. 137 sts.
Size 42/43: Complete border III, inc. likewise on each of the last 6 rows. 127 sts. Using C. work 4 rows then border I, inc. likewise. 139 sts.
All sizes: Cont. in C., k. 3 rows to form a p. stripe on right side. Cast off.

TO MAKE UP:

Darn in all loose ends. Omitting ribbing press work on wrong side with a hot iron over a damp cloth. Allow to dry. Join shoulders sewing through the p. stripe, leave 10 ins. open for neck. Slip st. around facing. Join sides and sleeves, edge to edge flat seams. Attach sleeves carefully matching centres to shoulders. Sew through the p. stripe and in second chain of sts. on Sweater. Press all seams.

LADY'S JACKET:

BACK:

Using no. 13 needles and Dg. cast on 120—130 sts. and work as for Sweater as far as second border III, inclusive. Cont. as follows:
Size 34/35 — 37/38: Complete the first 15—30 rows of border II then border I. All sizes: Cont. in Dg. k. 1 row then work each shoulder separately. P. 40—44 sts., turn, p. to end to form a stripe on right side, work 5 rows st.st. for facing. Cast off. Work the opposite shoulder to match. Cast off rem. sts. for neck.

LEFT FRONT:

Using no. 13 needles and Dg. cast on 72—77 sts. and work the welt as before, fin. on wrong side. Change to st.st. K. 60—65 sts., inc. 1 st., (to be worked in plain colour throughout) place rem. 12 sts. on a holder for Front Band. P. 1 row, inc. 1 st. at end of same. Change to no. 10 needles. Cont. in patt. to match Back. Having completed the second border III cont. as follows:
Size 37/38: Complete the first 15 rows of border II then shape neck.
Size 34/35 — 37/38: Work the first — last 15 rows of border II then border I. At the same time dec. at beg. of p. rows as follows: Cast off the seam st. then 5—6 sts. Then for all sizes 4 sts. once, 3 sts. twice, 2 sts. twice, 1 st. twice. 40—44 sts. rem. for shoulder. Cont. in Dg. k. 2 rows to form a stripe, work 5 rows st.st. for facing. Cast off.

RIGHT FRONT:

Work as for Left Front for ½ inch, fin. on wrong side. Next row: Rib 4 sts., cast off 5 sts. for buttonhole, rib to end. On next row cast on 5 sts. over those cast off. Complete the welt, fin. on right side. Change to st.st., beg. on a p. row. Work to last 12 sts., inc. 1 st., (to be worked in plain colour throughout) place the rem. 12 sts. on a holder for Front Band. K. 1 row, inc. 1 st. at end of same. Change to no. 10 needles. Cont. to match Left Front. Shape neck at beg. of k. rows.

SLEEVES:

Using no. 13 needles and Dg. cast on 60 sts., all sizes, work 1½—2 ins. in rib as before, fin. on wrong side. Change to st.st. Work 2 rows, inc. 1 st. at beg. of last row. Cont. in patt. Complete border I, then inc. as for Sweater sleeves until there are 101 sts. Complete borders II, III, II. Then rep. the first 15 rows of border III, inc. likewise on each of the last 10 rows. 121 sts. Complete border I, inc. likewise. 125 sts. Finally using Dg., k. 3 rows to form a stripe on right side. Cast off.

BUTTON BAND:

Using no. 13 needles and Dg. pick up the sts. from Left Front, inc. 1 st. at inner edge for seam. Cont. in rib until band reaches neckline, when slightly

stretched. Then cast off the seam st., leave rem. sts. on a holder. Attach to Front. Mark position of buttons, spacing evenly. Allow for one in neckband. (6 in all). Work buttonhole band to match making corresponding buttonholes.

TO MAKE UP:

Proceed as for Sweater.

NECKBAND:

Using no. 13 needles and Dg. pick up 119—123 sts. around neckline, right side facing and work 2½ ins. in rib as before. Make a buttonhole after ½ inch and again after 1¾ ins. Cast off ribwise. Fold on to wrong side and slip st. Sew around buttonholes. Attach buttons. Press well.

CIRCULAR KNITTING METHOD

MAN'S SWEATER:

BODY OF SWEATER:

Using circular needle no. 13 and C. cast on 280—300 sts. and work 1½ ins. in k. 1, p. 1 rib. Change to st.st. (k. all rds.) K. 1 rd. Change to circular needle no. 10. Cont. in patt. from chart, beg. as indicated. Complete borders I, II, III, II, III, II.
Size 38/40: Cont. in C., k. 4 rds., complete border I.
Size 42/43: Complete the first 15 rds. of border III, complete border I.
All sizes: Cont in C., k. 1 rd., p. 1 rd., k. 5 rds. for facing. Cast off.

SLEEVES:

Using set of needles no. 13 and C. cast on 70 sts., all sizes and work the welt as before. Change to st.st. K. 1 rd., inc. 1 st. at beg. of same. Change to set of no. 10 needles. Complete border I. Cont. in patt. Inc. 2 sts. at underarm, 1 st. either side of the first and last st. every 8th rd., working the extra sts. into patt., until there are 113—115 sts. Complete borders II, III, II. Then cont. as follows:
Size 38/40: Complete the first 32 rds. of border III, inc. likewise on each of the last 10 rds. 133 sts. Complete border I, inc. likewise. 137 sts.
Size 42/43: Complete border III, inc. likewise on each of the last 6 rds. 127 sts. Cont. in C. k. 4 rds., complete border I., inc. likewise. 139 sts.
All sizes: Using C., k. 1 rd., turn work inside out and k. 6 rds. for seam facing. Cast off.

TO MAKE UP:

Darn in all loose ends. Press. Allow to dry. Measure width of sleeve tops and mark corresponding length on Sweater for armholes. Machine twice around armholes to prevent fraying and cut between the machining. Join shoulders sewing through the p. stripe on right side. Leave 10 ins. open for neck. Slip st. around facing. Attach sleeves carefully matching centres to shoulders. Sew through the p. stripe and in chain of sts. just beyond the machining around armholes. Press seam, fold over raw edges on wrong side and slip st. to neaten. Press well.

LADY'S JACKET:

BODY OF JACKET:

Using circular needle no. 13 and Dg. cast on 265—285 sts. and work ½ inch in k. 1, p. 1 rib, to and fro. fin. on wrong side.

Next row: Rib. 4 sts., cast off 5 sts., for buttonhole, rib to end. On next row cast on 5 sts. over those cast off. Cont. until welt measures 1½ ins., fin. on wrong side. Next row: Rib 12 sts. for Front Band, place on a holder. K. to last 12 sts. and place these on a holder. Cast on 3 sts. and join the work into a rd. Work these sts. in plain colour throughout. The work is cut here later. 244—264 sts. Change to circular needle no. 10 and k. 1 rd.

Then cont. in border sequence as for Two Needle Method. Having completed the second border III cont. as follows. Shape neck: Size 34/35: On last rd. cast off the last 5 sts. also the centre 3 sts. From here work to and fro, p. on wrong side. Complete the first 15 rows of border II then border I. At the same time cast off at the beg. of each row 4 sts. once, 3 sts. twice, 2 sts. twice, 1 st. twice. 199 sts. rem.

Size 37/38: Work the first 15 rows of border II. On last rd. cast off the last 6 sts. also the centre 3 sts. Shape neck as for size 34/35. Complete the last 15 rows of border II also border I. 217 sts. rem.

All sizes: Cont. in Dg. as follows: K. 1 row. Allow the next 80—88 sts. for shoulders. P. 1 row on right side, work 5 rows st.st. for facing. Cast off the next 39—41 sts. for neck. Work rem. shoulders to match.

SLEEVES:

Using set of no. 13 needles and Dg. cast on 60 sts., all sizes. Work 1½—2 ins. in rib as before. Change to st.st. K. 2 rds., inc. 1 st. at beg. of last rd. Change to set of no. 10 needles. Cont. in patt. Complete border I. Then inc. as for Man's Sleeves until there are 101 sts. Cont. in border sequence as for Two Needle Method. Finally using Dg., k. 1 rd., turn sleeve inside out and k. 6 rds. for seam facing. Cast off.

BUTTON BAND:

Using no. 13 needles and Dg. cast on 5 sts. for facing then pick up the 12 sts. from Left Front. Cont. on these sts., working the 5 sts. in st.st. until the band reaches to neckline when slightly stretched. Then cast off the 5 sts., leave rem. sts. on a holder. Mark position of buttons, spacing evenly. Allow for one in neckband. (6 in all).

BUTTONHOLE BAND:

Work to match making corresponding buttonholes.

TO MAKE UP:

Proceed as for Sweater. Machine twice along centre 3 sts. and cut between the machining. Attach Front Bands.

NECKBAND:

As for Two Needle Method. Press well. Attach buttons.

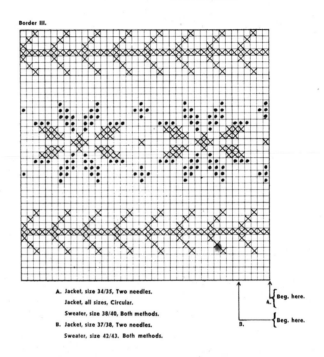

Border III.

A. Jacket, size 34/35, Two needles.
   Jacket, all sizes, Circular.
   Sweater, size 38/40, Both methods.
B. Jacket, size 37/38, Two needles.
   Sweater, size 42/43. Both methods.

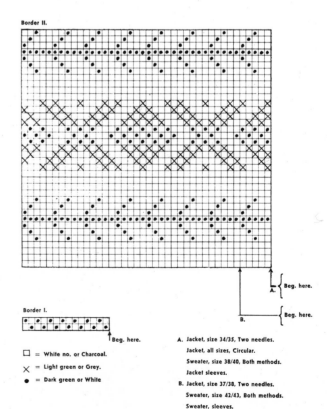

Border II.

A. Jacket, size 34/35, Two needles.
   Jacket, all sizes, Circular.
   Sweater, size 38/40, Both methods.
   Jacket sleeves.
B. Jacket, size 37/38, Two needles.
   Sweater, size 42/43, Both methods.
   Sweater, sleeves.

Border I.

Beg. here.

□ = White no. or Charcoal.
✕ = Light green or Grey.
● = Dark green or White

SHOWN IN COLOR ON INSIDE BACK COVER.

BOY'S OR MAN'S SWEATER

Size to fit 6-8-10-12 years, 38-40-42-44 inch chest.

Materials:

Size 6 8/10 12
  8   9   10 balls Blue no. 684.
  1   1   2 « Red no. 698.

38   40   42   44
14   15   16   17 balls Grey no. 689.
 2   2   2   2 « White no. 501.

A pair of needles each no. 10 and 13 or 2 circular needles and set of needles each no. 10 and 13.

American	SIZE OF NEEDLES	0	3
British		13	10

TENSION:

26 stitches and 34 rows on no. 10 needles = 4 inches.
Check your tension very carefully. Adjust by using thicker or thinner needles.

ABBREVIATIONS:

Beg., beginning; cont., continue; fin., finishing; inc., increase; inc. 1 st., pick up loop between sts. and k. into back of same; k., knit; patt., pattern; p., purl; rem., remaining; rd., round; sts., stitches; st.st., stocking stitch; Mc., Main colour. **Mens sizes are in parentheses.**

TWO NEEDLE METHOD

BACK AND FRONT ALIKE:

Using no. 13 needles and Mc. cast on 96—102—108—114 (132—138—144—150) sts. and work 1½ ins. in k. 1, p. 1 rib, fin on wrong side. Change to no. 10 needles and st.st. (k. on right, p. on wrong side). Inc. 1 st. at beg. of first row. x. When entire work measures 15—16½—18—20 (25—26—26½—27½) ins., fin. on wrong side, complete the border from chart. Finally p. 1 row on right side, work 5 (6) rows st.st. for facing. Cast off.

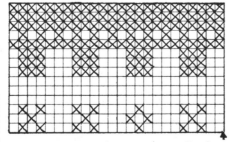

□ = Blue or grey.
✗ = Red or white.

Beg. here.

SLEEVES:

Two sets of figures only, denote the first and last two sizes. Using no. 13 needles and Mc. cast on 56—56—60—62 (70—74) sts. and work as Back as far as x. Inc. 1 st. within the first and last st. every 8th row until there are 79—85—91—97 (109—115) sts. When entire sleeve measures 12—13—14½—15 (18—19) ins., fin. on wrong side, complete the border. Inc. likewise on each of the last 10 rows (every row). 99—105—111—117 (137—143) sts. Finally p. 2 rows. Cast off.

TO MAKE UP:

Darn in all loose ends. Press work on wrong side with a hot iron over a damp cloth. Allow to dry. Join shoulders sewing through the p. stripe. Leave 8 (10) ins. open for neck. Slip st. around facing. Join sides and sleeves, edge to edge flat seams. Attach sleeves carefully matching centres to shoulders. Sew through the p. stripe and in second chain of sts. on Sweater. Press all seams.

CIRCULAR KNITTING METHOD

BODY OF SWEATER:

Using circular needle no. 13 and Mc. cast on 192—204—216—228 (264—276—288—300) sts. and work 1½ ins. in k. 1, p. 1 rib. Change to st.st., k. all rds. K. 1 rd. Change to circular needle no. 10. x. When entire work measures 15—16½—18—20 (25—26—26½—27½) ins. complete the border from chart. Finally p. 1 rd., k. 5 (6) rds. for facing. Cast off.

SLEEVES:

Two sets of figures only, denote the first and last two sizes. Using set of needles no. 13 and Mc. cast on 56—56—60—62 (70—74) sts. and work as Sweater as far as x. Cont. in st.st., inc. 1 st. at beg. of first rd. Further inc. 2 sts. at underarm, 1 st. either side of first and last st. every 8th rd. until there are 79—85—91—97 (109—115) sts. When entire sleeve measures 12—13—14½—15 (18—19) ins., complete the border. Inc. likewise on each of the last 10 rds. (every rd.). 99—105—111—117 (137—143) sts. Then turn the sleeve inside out and k. 6 rds. for seam facing. Cast off.

TO MAKE UP:

Darn in all loose ends. Press. Allow to dry. Measure width of sleeve tops and mark corresponding length on Sweater for armholes. Make sure that patts. match at both sides. Machine twice around armholes, to prevent fraying and cut between the machining. Join shoulders sewing through the p. stripe on right side. Leave 8 (10) ins. open for neck. Slip st. around facing. Attach sleeves carefully matching centres to shoulders. Sew through the p. stripe and in chain of sts. just beyond the machining around armholes. Press seam. Fold facing over raw edges on wrong side and slip st. to neaten. Press well.

SHOWN IN COLOR ON PAGE 24.

LADY'S JUMPER AND MAN'S JACKET

Size to fit 34-36-38-39 inch bust, 40-42 inch chest.

Materials:

Size	34	36	38	39		40/42
	6	6	7	7	balls Blue no. 671.	9 balls Dark grey no. 9.
	4	5	5	6	« Light blue no. 707.	6 « Grey no. 582.
	5	6	6	6	« White no. 501.	7 « White no. 501.

A pair of needles each no. 10 and 13 or 2 circular and set of needles each no. 10 and 13.

American	SIZE OF NEEDLES	0	3
British		13	10

TENSION:

26 stitches and 30 rows in pattern on no. 10 needles = 4 inches.
Check your tension very carefully. Adjust by using thicker or thinner needles.

ABBREVIATIONS:

Beg., beginning; cont., continue; dec., decrease; fin., finishing; inc., increase; inc. 1 st., pick up loop between sts. and k. into back of same; k., knit; patt., pattern; p., purl; rem., remaining; rep., repeat; rd., round; sts., stitches; st. st., stocking stitch; Mc., Main colour.

LADY'S JUMPER:

Two sets of figures only, denote the first and last two sizes.

BACK AND FRONT ALIKE:

Using no. 13 needles and Mc. cast on 126—136 sts. and work 1½ ins. in k. 1, p. 1 rib, fin. on wrong side. Change to st. st. (k. on right, p. on wrong side). Work 2 rows, inc. 1 st. at end of last row. Change to no. 10 needles. Cont. in patt. from chart, beg. as

indicated. x. Complete borders i and II three times. xx. Rep. border I omitting the last 5 rows. Cont. in Mc., k. 1 row, p. 1 row on right side to form a stripe, work 6 rows st. st. for facing. Cast off.

SLEEVES:

Using no. 13 needles and Mc. cast on 60 sts., all sizes. Work as Back as far as x. Then inc. 1 st. within the first and last st. every 8th row until there are 101 sts., working the extra sts. into patt. Complete borders III and II (omitting the last 3 rows of border II) three times. xx. Then rep. the first 11 rows of border III, inc. likewise on each row. 123 sts. Finally using Mc., k. 2 rows to form a stripe. Cast off.

TO MAKE UP:

Darn in all loose ends. Omitting ribbing press work on wrong side with a hot iron over a damp cloth. Allow to dry. Join shoulders sewing through the p. stripe, leave 9 ins. open for neck. Slip st. around facing. Join sides and sleeves, edge to edge flat seams. Attach sleeves

carefully matching centres to shoulders. Sew through the p. stripe and in second chain of sts. on Jumper. Press all seams.

MAN'S JACKET:

BACK:

Using no. 13 needles and Mc. cast on 144 sts. Work as for Back of Lady's Jumper as far as xx. Complete border IV. Then work each shoulder separately. Allow 50 sts. for each. P. 1 row on right side to form a stripe, work 5 rows st. st. for facing. Cast off shoulders and rem. 45 sts. for neck.

RIGHT FRONT:

Using no. 13 needles and Mc. cast on 84 sts. and work the welt as before, fin. on wrong side. Next row: Place the first 12 sts. on a holder for Front Band, change to st. st. Work 2 rows, inc. 1 st. at end of each for seam and work the st. next to Front Band in plain colour throughout. Change to no. 10 needles. Cont. in patt. to match Back. Having completed the third border II shape neck. Keeping continuity of border IV cast off the seam st., then 6 sts., k. to end. Further dec. at beg. of k. rows, 5, 4, 3 twice, 2 sts., until 50 sts. rem. for shoulder. Complete as for Back.

LEFT FRONT:

Work as for RIGHT FRONT for 1 inch, fin. on right side. Next row: Rib 4, cast off 5 sts. for buttonhole, rib to end. On next row cast on 5 sts. over those cast off. Complete the welt, fin. on wrong side. Change to st. st. K. 72 sts., inc. 1 st. for seam, leave rem. 12 sts. on a holder. P. 1 row, inc. 1 st. at end of same. Work to match Right Front. Shape neck at beg. of p. rows.

SLEEVES:

Using no. 13 needles and Mc. cast on 72 sts. Work as for Lady's Sleeves as far as xx but inc. to 115 sts. Having completed the third border II rep. border III, complete border IV, inc. likewise on each row. Finally p. 1 row on right side to form a stripe, k. 1 row. Cast off.

BUTTON BAND:

Using no. 13 needles and Mc. pick up the sts. from Right Front, inc. 1 st. at inner edge for seam. Cont. in rib until band when slightly stretched reaches neckline. Cast off the seam st. and leave rem. sts. on a holder. Attach to Front. Mark position of buttons, spacing evenly. Allow for 1 in neckband. (6 in all.)

BUTTONHOLE BAND:

Work to match making corresponding buttonholes as before. Attach to Front.

TO MAKE UP:

Proceed as for Jumper.

NECKBAND:

Using no. 13 needles and Mc. pick up the sts. from Right Band, 119 sts. around neckline and sts. from Left Band. Work 2½ ins. in rib as before. Make a buttonhole after ½ inch and again after 1½ ins. Cast off ribwise. Fold on to wrong side and slip st. Sew around buttonholes. Attach buttons.

CIRCULAR KNITTING METHOD

LADY'S JUMPER:
BODY OF JUMPER:
Using circular needle no. 13 and Mc. cast on 252—270 sts. and work 1½ ins. in k. 1, p. 1 rib. Change to st. st. (k. all rds.). K. 1 rd. Change to circular needle no. 10. Cont. in patt. from chart, beg. as indicated. Work in border sequence as for Two Needle Method. Finally using Mc. k. 1 rd., p. 1 rd., k. 6 rds. for facing. Cast off.

SLEEVES:
Using set of needles no. 13 and Mc. cast on 60 sts., all sizes. Work 1½ ins. in rib as before. K. 1 rd. Change to set of needles no. 10. Inc. 2 sts. at underarm, 1 st. either side of the first and last st. every 8th rd. until there are 101 sts. Work in border sequence as for Two Needle Method and same shaping. Finally using Mc. k. 1 rd., turn sleeve inside out and k. 6 rds. for seam facing. Cast off.

TO MAKE UP:
Darn in all loose ends. Press. Measure width of sleeve tops and mark corresponding length on Jumper for armholes. Make sure that patts. match at armholes. Machine twice around armholes, to prevent fraying and cut between the machining. Join shoulders sewing though the p. stripe on right side. Leave 9 ins. open for neck. Slip st. around facing. Attach sleeves carefully matching centres to shoulders. Sew through the p. stripe and in chain of sts. just beyond the machining around armholes. Press seam, fold facing over raw edges on wrong side and slip st. to neaten. Press well.

MAN'S JACKET:
BODY OF JACKET:
Using circular needle no. 13 and Mc. cast on 313 sts. and work 1 inch in k. 1, p. 1 rib, to and fro, fin. on right side. Next row: Rib 4, cast off 5 sts. for buttonhole, rib to end. On next row cast on 5 sts. over those cast off. Cont. in rib until welt measures 1½ ins., fin. on wrong side. Next row: Rib 12 sts., place on a holder for Front Band, change to circular needle no. 10 and st. st., k. to last 12 sts., place on a holder. Then cast on 3 sts. and join work into a rd. Work these in plain colour throughout. The work is cut here later. Cont. in same border sequence as for Two Needle Method. On last rd. of the third border II shape neck. Cast off the last 6 sts. and the centre 3 sts. Keeping continuity of border IV cast off the first 6 sts., k. to end. From here work to and fro, p. on wrong side. Then cast off at beg. of every row 5, 4, 3 twice, 2 sts. until 243 sts. rem. Cont. in Mc. and work the shoulders separately. Allow 50 sts. for each. P. 1 row on right side to form a stripe, work 5 rows st. st. for facing. Cast off shoulders and rem. 43 sts. for neck.

SLEEVES:
Using set of needles no. 13 and Mc. cast on 72 sts. and work the welt as before. K. 1 rd., inc. 1 st. at beg. of same. K. 1 rd. Change to set of needles

no. 10. Inc. 2 sts. at underarm, 1 st. either side of the first and last st. every 8th rd. until there are 115 sts. Work in border sequence as for Two Needle Method and same shaping. Finally using Mc., k. 1 rd., turn sleeve inside out and k. 6 rds. for seam facing. Cast off.

BUTTON BAND:
Using no. 13 needles and Mc. cast on 5 sts. for facing, then pick up the 12 sts. from Right Front. Cont. in rib but work the facing in st. st., until band when slightly stretched reaches to neckline. Then cast off the 5 sts., leave rem. sts. on a holder. Mark position of buttons, spacing evenly, allow for 1 in neckband. (6 in all.)

BUTTONHOLE BAND:
Work to match making corresponding buttonholes as before.

TO MAKE UP:
Proceed as for Jumper. Machine twice along centre front and cut between the machining. Attach Front Bands. Press seam, fold facing over raw edges on wrong side and slip st. to neaten.

NECKBAND:
As for Two Needle Method. Press well. Attach buttons.

Border II

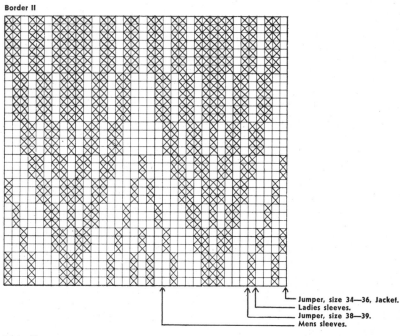

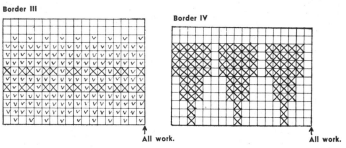

Jumper, size 34—36, Jacket.
Ladies sleeves.
Jumper, size 38—39.
Mens sleeves.

Border III

All work.

Border IV

All work.

□ = Blue or Dark grey.
X = White.
v = Light blue or Grey.

Border I

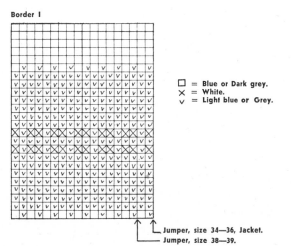

Jumper, size 34—36, Jacket.
Jumper, size 38—39.

SHOWN IN COLOR ON PAGE 24.

LADY'S OR MAN'S SWEATER

Size to fit 32-34-35-36 inch bust, 38-40-41-42 inch chest

Materials:

Size	32	34	35/36		
	9	10	11	balls	Light blue no. 707.
	3	3	4	«	Blue no. 671.
	3	3	3	«	White no. 501.
	1	1	1	ball	Black no. 502.

Size	38	40	41	42	
	12	12	13	13	balls Grey no. 5.
	4	4	4	5	« Dark grey no. 7.
	3	4	4	4	« White no. 501.
	1	1	1	1	ball Red no. 681.

A pair of needles each no. 10 and 13 or 2 circular needles and set of needles each no. 10 and 13.

Actual measurements:

Size	32	34	35	36	38	40	41	42		
All round	36	36	38½	38½	42	42	45	45	ins. approx.
Length	24½	24½	26	27	27	27½	28	29	«	«
Sleeve seam	19	19	19½	20	21	21	22	22	«	«

American		SIZE OF NEEDLES	0	3
British			13	10

TENSION:

26 stitches and 30 rows in pattern on no. 10 needles = 4 inches.
Check your tension very carefully. Adjust by using thicker or thinner needles.

ABBREVIATIONS:

Beg., beginning; cont., continue; dec., decrease; fin., finishing; inc., increase; inc. 1 st., pick up loop between sts. and k. into back of same; k., knit; patt., pattern; p., purl; rem., remaining; rd., round; sts., stitches; st.st., stocking stitch; Dg., Dark grey; Mc., Main colour.

TWO NEEDLE METHOD

Two sets of figures only, denote the first and last two sizes. Man's sizes are in parentheses.

BACK AND FRONT ALIKE:

Using no. 13 needles and Mc. (Dg.) cast on 120—128 (140—148) sts. and work 1½ ins. (4 rows, 1½ ins. in Mc.), in k. 1, p. 1 rib, fin on wrong side. Change to st.st., k. on right, p. on wrong side. Work 2 rows, inc. 1 st. at beg. of last row. Change to no. 10 needles. x. Cont. in main patt., from chart, beg. as indicated until entire work measures 16—17—17½—18 (18½—19—20—21) ins., fin. on a patt. row. Then complete borders I and II. Finally p. 1 row on right side to form a stripe, work 5 (6) rows st.st. for facing. Cast off.

SLEEVES:

Using no. 13 needles and Mc. (Dg.) cast on 64 (72) sts. and work as far as x. Cont. in main patt. Inc. 1 st. within the first and last st. every 8th row until there are 87—89 (97—101) sts. When entire work measures 10½—11—11—12 (12½—13—13½—14) ins., fin. on a patt. row, complete borders I and II. Inc. likewise every 6th row. 109—111 (117—121) sts. Inc. likewise on each of the rem. 12 rows. Finally p. 2 rows or k. 2 rows to form a stripe. Cast off.

TO MAKE UP:

Darn in all loose ends. Omitting ribbing press work on wrong side with a hot iron over a damp cloth. Allow to dry. Join shoulders sewing through the p. stripe. Leave 9 (10) ins. open for neck. Slip st. around facing. Join sides and sleeves, edge to edge flat seams. Attach sleeves carefully matching centres to shoulders. Sew through the p. stripe and in second chain of sts. on Sweater. Press all seams.

Border II

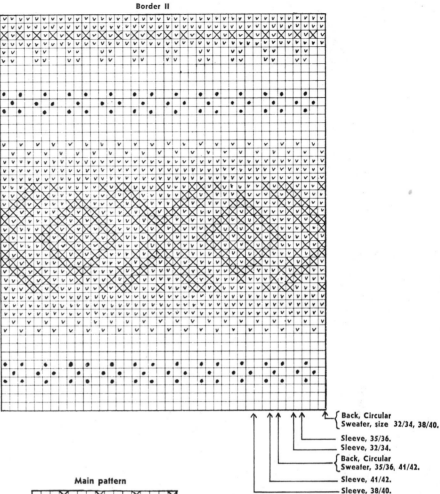

Back, Circular Sweater, size 32/34, 38/40.
Sleeve, 35/36.
Sleeve, 32/34.
Back, Circular Sweater, 35/36, 41/42.
Sleeve, 41/42.
Sleeve, 38/40.

Border I

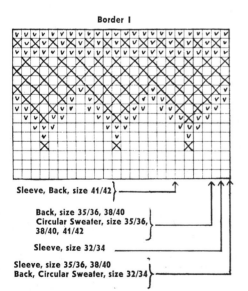

Sleeve, Back, size 41/42
Back, size 35/36, 38/40 Circular Sweater, size 35/36, 38/40, 41/42
Sleeve, size 32/34
Sleeve, size 35/36, 38/40 Back, Circular Sweater, size 32/34

Main pattern

☐ = Light blue or grey.
✕ = White.
v = Blue or Dark grey.
● = Black or red.

CIRCULAR KNITTING METHOD

Using circular needle no. 13 and Mc. (Dg.) cast on 240—264 (280—296) sts. and work 1½ ins. (4rds., 1½ ins. in Mc.). Change to st.st., k. all rds. K. 1 rd. Change to circular needle no. 10. Cont. in main patt., from chart, beg. as indicated, until entire work measures 16—17—18—18½ (18½—19—20—21) ins., fin. on a patt. rd. Then complete border I. Cont. with border II. Size 35/36 and 41/42: Dec. (inc.) 4 sts. evenly on second rd. Finally p. 1 rd., k. 5 (6) rds. for facing. Cast off.

SLEEVES:

Using set of needles no. 13 and Mc. (Dg) cast on 64 (72) sts. and work the welt as before. K. 1 rd., inc. 1 st. at beg. of same. Change to set of needles no. 10. Cont. in main patt. Inc. 2 sts. at underarm, 1 st. either side of the first and last st. every 8th rd. until there are 87—89 (97—101) sts. When entire sleeve measures 10½—11—11½—12 (12½—13—13½—14) ins., fin. on a patt. rd., complete borders I and II. Inc. likewise every 6th rd. 109—111 (117—121) sts. Inc. likewise on each of the rem. 12 rds. Finally turn work inside out and k. 6 rds. for seam facing. Cast off.

TO MAKE UP:

Darn in all loose ends. Press. Measure width of sleeve tops and mark corresponding length on Sweater for armholes. Place beg. of rds. at one side. Machine twice around armholes to prevent fraying and cut between the machining. Join shoulders sewing through the p. stripe on right side of work. Leave 9 (10) ins. open for neck. Slip st. around facing. Attach sleeves carefully matching centres to shoulders. Sew through the first p. rd. and in chain of sts. just beyond the machining around armholes. Press seam, fold facing over raw edges on wrong side and slip st. to neaten. Press well.

15

SHOWN IN COLOR ON PAGE 25.

LADY'S OR MAN'S SWEATER

Size to fit 32-34 / 36-38 inch bust, 38-40 / 42-44 inch chest.

Materials:

Size 32	34/36	38		38	40/42	44		
8	8	9		9	10	11	balls	White no. 501 or 17.
4	4	4		4	4	5	«	Grey no. 2.
3	3	3		3	4	4	«	Black no. 502.
2	2	2		3	3	3	«	Green no. 734.
1	1	1					ball	Red no. 681.

A pair of needles each no. 10 and 13 or 2 circular needles and set of needles each no. 10 and 13.

American				SIZE OF NEEDLES	0	3
British					13	10

TENSION:

26 stitches and 30 rows in pattern on no. 10 needles = 4 inches. **Check your tension very carefully. Adjust by using thicker or thinner needles.**

ABBREVIATIONS:

Beg., beginning; cont., continue; fin., finishing; inc., increase; inc. 1 st., pick up loop between sts. and k. into back of same; k., knit; patt., pattern; p., purl; rem., remaining; rd., round; rep., repeat; sts., stitches; st.st., stocking stitch; B. Black.

TWO NEEDLE METHOD

LADIES SWEATER:
BACK AND FRONT ALIKE:

Using no. 13 needles and B. cast on 120—120 / 132—132 sts. and work 1 inch in k. 1, p. 1 rib, fin. on right side. P. 1 row, inc. 1 st. at end of same. Change to no. 10 needles and st. st. (k. on right, p. on wrong side). Cont. in patt. from chart, beg. as indicated. x Complete border I, cont. in main patt. for 14—15—16 ins., fin. with a complete design. Complete border II, rep. the first 9 rows of main patt., entire border I. Finally p. 1 row on right side to form a stripe, work 5 rows st. st. for facing. Cast off.

SLEEVES:

Using no. 13 needles and B. cast on 64 sts., all sizes, and work as for Sweater as far as x. Then inc. 1 st. within the first and last st. every 8th row, working the extra sts. into patt. until there are 99—101—103 sts. Work in same border sequence as for Sweater with 7½—8½—9½ ins. in main patt. prior to border II. Inc. likewise on the 3rd and 6th row and on each of the last 12 rows of upper border I. 127—129—131 sts. Finally p. or k. 2 rows to form a stripe on right side. Cast off.

TO MAKE UP:

Darn in all loose ends. Omitting ribbing press work on wrong side with a hot iron over a damp cloth. Allow to dry. Join shoulders sewing through the p. stripe on right side. Leave 9 ins. open for neck. Slip st. around facing. Join sides and sleeves, edge to edge flat seams. Attach sleeves carefully matching centres to shoulders. Sew through the p. stripe and in second chain of sts. on Sweater. Press all seams.

MENS SWEATER:
BACK:

Using no. 13 needles and B. cast on 132—144—156 sts. and work as Lady's Sweater to x. Complete border I, cont. in main patt. for 18—18/19—20 ins., fin. with a complete design, rep. border I. Then work the shoulders separately. Allow 44—49—54 sts. for each. P. 1 row on right side to form a stripe, work 5 rows st. st. for facing. Cast off shoulders and rem. sts. for neck.

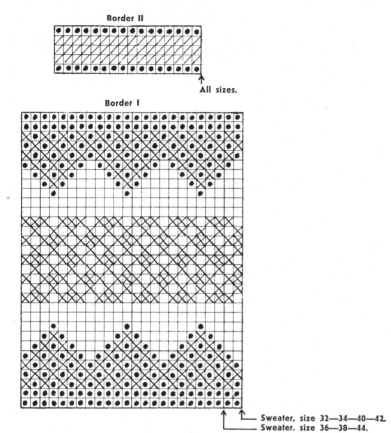

Border II

All sizes.

Border I

Sweater, size 32—34—40—42.
Sweater, size 36—38—44.

Main pattern.

Sweater, size 32—34—40—42.
Sweater, size 36—38—44.
Sleeves all sizes.

□ = White
● = Black.
✕ = Green
ᴠ = Grey.
╱ = Red.

FRONT:

Work as Back as far as 12th row of upper border I then shape neck. K. the first 61—66—71 sts., turn. Cast off at beg. of p. rows, 3 sts. twice, 2 sts. thrice, 1 st. 5 times until 44—49—54 sts. rem. for shoulder. Complete as before. Cast off the centre 11—13—15 sts. and work the opposite side to match.

SLEEVES:

Using no. 13 needles and B. cast on 72 sts., all sizes. Work as for Lady's Sleeves omitting border II. Inc. likewise to 109—111—113 sts. and work 14—14½—15 ins. in main patt. Inc. on the 2nd, 4th and 6th row and on each of the last 12 rows of upper border I. 139—141—143 sts.

TO MAKE UP:

As for Lady's Sweater.

NECKBAND:

Using no. 13 needles and B. cast on 136—140—144 sts. and work 2½ ins. in rib as before. Cast off loosely, rib-wise. Attach to neckline, fold in half and slip st. on wrong side.

CIRCULAR KNITTING METHOD

LADY'S SWEATER:
BODY OF SWEATER:

Using circular needle no. 13 and B. cast on 240—240 / 264—264 sts. and work 1 inch in k. 1, p. 1 rib. Change to circular needle no. 10 and st. st. (k. all

rds.). K. 1 rd. Cont. in patt. from chart, beg. as indicated. Work in border sequence as for Two Needle Method. Finally p. 1 rd., k. 6 rds. for facing. Cast off.

SLEEVES:

Using set of needles no. 13 and B. cast on 64 sts., all sizes. Work the welt as before. Change to set of needles no. 10 and st. st. K. 1 rd., inc. 1 st. at end of same. Cont. in border sequence as for Two Needle Method, inc. likewise. Finally turn sleeve inside out and k. 6 rds. for seam facing. Cast off.

TO MAKE UP:

Darn in all loose ends. Press. Measure width of sleeve tops and mark corresponding length on Sweater for armholes. Machine twice around armholes, to prevent fraying, in chain of sts. and cut between the machining. Join shoulders sewing through the p. stripe on right side. Leave 9 ins. open for neck. Slip st. around facing. Attach sleeves carefully matching centres to shoulders. Sew through the p. stripe and in chain of sts. just beyond the machining around armholes. Press seam, fold facing over raw edges on wrong side and slip st. to neaten. Press well.

MAN'S SWEATER:
BODY OF SWEATER:

Using circular needle no. 13 and B. cast on 264—288—312 sts. and work 1 inch in k. 1, p. 1 rib. Change to circular needle no. 10 and st. st. (k. all rds.). K. 1 rd. Cont. in border sequence as for Two needle Method. On 12th rd. of upper border I shape neck. Keeping continuity of patt., k. 60—65—70 sts., cast off 12—14—16 sts. for neck, k. to beg. of neckline. From here work to and fro, p. on wrong side. Cast off at beg. of each row 3 sts. twice, 2 sts. thrice, 1 st. 5 times. Finally work the shoulders separately. Allow 86—96—106 sts. either side of the neck. P. 1 row on right side to form a stripe, work 5 rows st. st. for facing. Cast off shoulders and rem. sts. for neck.

SLEEVES:

Using set of needles no. 13 and B. cast on 72 sts., all sizes. Work as for Lady's Sleeves omitting border II. Work in same border sequence with same shapings as for Two Needle Method.

TO MAKE UP:

As for Lady's Sweater.

NECKBAND:

Using set of needles no. 13 and B. pick up 136—140—144 sts. around neckline and work 2½ ins. in rib as before. Cast off loosely, ribwise. Fold in half and slip st. on wrong side.

SHOWN IN COLOR ON INSIDE FRONT COVER.

LADY'S, MAN'S, AND CHILD'S JACKETS

Size to fit 34-35-36-38 inch bust, 38-40-42-44 inch chest, 8-10-12-14 years.

A pair of needles each no. 10 and 13 or 2 circular needles and set of needles each no. 10 and 13.

American		SIZE OF NEEDLES	0	3
British			13	10

Materials:

Size 34/35 36/38
      13   14   balls White no. 17.
       4   5   «   Black no. 502.

38   40   42   44
14   16   16   16 balls Charcoal no. 12.
 5   5   6   6 «   White no. 17.

Size 8 10/12 14
     10   12   13 balls Blue no. 671.
      3   4   4 «   White no. 501
                          or 17.

TENSION:

26 stitches and 32 rows in main (30 in border) pattern on no. 10 needles = 4 inches.

Check your tension very carefully. Adjust by using thicker or thinner needles.

ABBREVIATIONS:

Beg., beginning; cont., continue; dec., decrease; fin., finishing; inc., increase; inc. 1 st., pick up loop between sts. and k. into back of same; k., knit; Mc., Main Colour; patt., pattern; p., purl; rem., remaining; rd., round; st.st., stocking stitch.

TWO NEEDLE METHOD

LADY'S AND GIRL'S JACKET:
Two sets of figures only, denoting the first and last two sizes.
Girl's sizes are in parentheses.

BACK:

Using no. 13 needles and Mc. cast on 120—134 (100—114—114—120) sts. and work 1½ ins. in k. 1, p. 1 rib, fin. on wrong side. Change to st.st., k. on right,

p. on wrong side. Work 2 rows, inc. 1 st. at end of last row. Change to no. 10 needles. x. Cont. in patt. from chart, beg. as indicated. Complete border I, cont. in main patt. 12—12½—13—14 (7—9—10½—12½) ins., ending on a patt. (5th plain) row, complete border II, beg. at 16th row for Girls. Cont. in Mc., work 1 row. Then work each shoulder separately. Allow 41—47 (35—39—39—41) sts. for each. P. 1 row on right side to form a stripe, work 5 rows st.st. for facing, cast off. Cast off rem. sts. for neck.

LEFT FRONT:

Using no. 13 needles and Mc. cast on 73—80(62—69—69—72)sts. and work 1½ ins. in rib as before, fin. on wrong side. Change to st.st. K. 60—67 (50—57—57—60) sts., inc. 1 st. for seam, place rem. 13 (12) sts. on a holder for Front Band. P. 1 row, inc. 1 st. at end of same Work the seam st. in plain colour throughout. Cont. in patt. to match Back. On 51st (38th) row of border II shape neck, beg. on a p. row. Keeping continuity of patt. cast off the seam st. then 4—5 (4—5—5—6) sts., p. to end. Further dec. at beg. of p. rows, all sizes, 4 sts. once, 3 sts. twice, 2 sts. twice, 1 st.

18

twice (3—4—4—4 sts. twice, all sizes, 2 sts. twice, 1 st. twice) until 41—47 (35—39—39—41) sts. rem. for shoulder. Cont. in Mc., k. or p. 2 rows to form a stripe, work 5 rows in st.st. for facing. Cast off.

RIGHT FRONT:

Work as Left Front for 1 inch, fin on wrong side. Next row: Rib to last 9 sts., cast off 5 sts. for buttonhole, rib to end. On next row cast on 5 sts. over those cast off. Complete the welt to match Left Front, fin. on right side. Change to st.st. Cont. to match Left Front, beg. on a p. row. Reverse neck shapings, on k. rows.

SLEEVES:

Using no. 13 needles and Mc. cast on 64 sts., all sizes (54—60) sts. and work as Back to x. Then inc. 1 st. within the first and last st. every 8th row until there are 91—93 (81—85—95—97) sts. Complete border I, cont. in main patt. 9—10 (5½—7—8—9½) ins., fin. as before, complete the first 37 rows (16th—37th) row of border II. Inc. likewise. 103—105 (81—85—95—97) sts. Then complete border III, inc. likewise on every row (last 10 rows). 125—127 (101—105—115—117) sts. Finally using Mc., k. or p. 3 rows to form a stripe. Cast off.

BUTTON BAND:

Using no. 13 needles and Mc. pick up the 13 (12) sts. from Left Front, cast on 1 st. at inner edge for seam. Cont. in rib until Band when slightly stretched reaches neckline. Then cast off the seam st., leave rem. sts. on a holder. Attach to Front. Mark position of buttons, spacing evenly. Allow for one in neckband. 6 (5) in all. Work the Buttonhole Band to match making corresponding buttonholes.

Border I

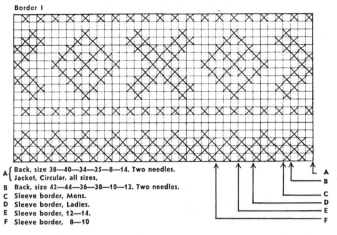

A { Back, size 38—40—34—35—8—14. Two needles.
Jacket, Circular. all sizes.
B Back, size 42—44—36—38—10—12. Two needles.
C Sleeve border, Mens.
D Sleeve border, Ladies.
E Sleeve border, 12—14.
F Sleeve border, 8—10

Border II

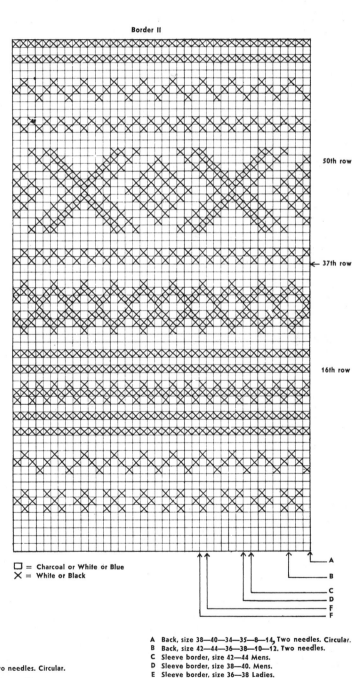

50th row

37th row

16th row

□ = Charcoal or White or Blue
X = White or Black

A Back, size 38—40—34—35—8—14. Two needles. Circular.
B Back, size 42—44—36—38—10—12. Two needles.
C Sleeve border, size 42—44 Mens.
D Sleeve border, size 38—40. Mens.
E Sleeve border, size 36—38 Ladies.
F Sleeve border, size 34—35. Ladies.

Border III

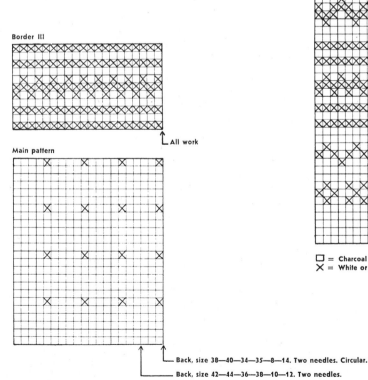

All work

Main pattern

Back, size 38—40—34—35—8—14. Two needles. Circular.
Back, size 42—44—36—38—10—12. Two needles.

19

TO MAKE UP:

Darn in all loose ends. Omitting ribbing press work on wrong side with a hot iron over a damp cloth. Allow to dry. Join shoulders sewing through the p. stripe. Slip st. around facing. Join sides and sleeves, edge to edge flat seams. Attach sleeves carefully matching centres to shoulders. Sew through the p. stripe and in second chain of sts. on Jacket. Press all seams.

NECKBAND:

Using no. 13 needles and Mc. pick up the 13 (12) sts. from Right Front Band, 103—105—109—109 (91—93—95—101) sts. around neckline, the 13 (12) sts. from Left Front Band. Work 2½ ins. in rib as before. Make a buttonhole after ½ inch again after 1½ ins. Cast off loosely. Sew around buttonholes. Attach buttons.

MAN'S AND BOY'S JACKET:

Two sets of figures only, denoting the first and last two sizes.
Boy's sizes are in parentheses.

Using no. 13 needles and Mc. cast on 140 —154(100—114—114—120) sts. and work as Ladies Jacket to x. Cont. in patt. from chart, beg. as indicated. Complete border I, cont. in main patt. 14—14½—15 —16 (7—9—10½—12½) ins. fin. on a patt. (5th plain) row, complete border II. Beg. at 16th row for Boys. Cont. in Mc., work 1 row. Then work each shoulder separately. Allow 50—55 (35—39—39— 41) sts. for each. P. 1 row on right side, work 5 rows st.st. for facing, cast off. Cast off rem. sts. for neck.

RIGHT FRONT:

Using no. 13 needles and Mc. cast on 82—89 (62—69—69—72) sts. and work the welt as before, fin. on right side. Change to st.st. P. 70—77 (50—57—57 —60) sts., inc. 1 st. for seam, place rem. 12 sts. on a holder for Front Band. K. 1 row, inc. 1 st. at end of same. Work the seam st. in plain colour throughout. Cont. to match Back. On 51st (38th) row of border II shape neck, beg. on a k. row. Keeping continuity of patt. cast off the seam st. then 5—6 (4—5—5—6) sts., k. to end. Further dec. at beg. of k. rows 3—4 sts., then for all sizes, 3 sts. twice, 2 sts. thrice, 1 st. once (3—4—4—4 sts. twice, then for all sizes, 2 sts. twice, 1 st. twice) until 50—55 (35—39—39—41) sts. rem. for shoulder. Cont. in Mc., k. or p. 2 rows to form a stripe, work 5 rows st.st. for facing. Cast off.

LEFT FRONT:

Work as Right Front for 1 inch, fin. on wrong side. Next row: Rib to last 9 sts., cast off 5 sts. for buttonhole, rib to end. On next row cast on 5 sts. over those cast off. Complete the welt to match Right Front, fin. on wrong side. Change to st.st. Cont. to match Right Front, beg. on a k. row. Reverse neck shapings, on p. rows.

SLEEVES:

Using no. 13 needles and Mc. cast on 72 sts., all sizes (54—60) sts. and work as Back to x. Then inc. 1 st. within the first and last st. every 8th row, working the extra sts. into patt., until there are 103—105 (81—85—95—97) sts. Complete border I, cont. in main patt. 10—10½— 11—11½ (5½—7—8—9½) ins., fin. as before, complete the first 37 rows (16— 37 row) of border II. Inc. likewise. 115— 117 (81—85—95—97) sts. Then complete border III, inc. likewise on every row (last 10 rows). 137—139 (101—105 —115—117) sts. Finally using Mc., k. or p. 3 rows to form a stripe. Cast off.

TO MAKE UP:

As for Lady's Jacket.

NECKBAND:

Pick up the sts. from Front Bands and 117—119 (91—93—95—101) sts. around neckline.

CIRCULAR KNITTING METHOD

LADY'S AND GIRL'S JACKET:

Using circular needle no. 13 and Mc. cast on 267—287 (225—245—245—265) sts. and work 1 inch in k. 1, p. 1 rib, to and fro, fin. on wrong side. Next row: Rib 4, cast off 5 sts. for buttonhole, rib to end. On next row cast on 5 sts. over those cast off. Cont. until welt measures 1½ ins., fin. on wrong side. Next row: Rib 13 (12) sts., place on a holder for Front Band, change to st.st., k. all rds. K. to last 13 (12) sts., place on a holder. Change to circular needle no. 10. Cast on 3 sts. and join the work into a rd. Work these sts. in plain colour throughout. The work is cut here later. Cont. in patt. as for Two Needle Method. On 50th (37th) rd. of border II shape neck thus: Cast off the last 4—5 (4—4 —4—5) sts., also the centre 3 sts. Next rd.: Cast off the first 4—5 (4—4—4—5) sts., k. to end. From here work to and fro, p. on wrong side. Keeping continuity of patt. cast off at beg. of each row, all sizes, 4 sts. once, 3 sts. twice, 2 sts. once, 1 st. thrice (3— 4—4—4 sts., next time 2—3—3—4 sts., then all sizes, 2 sts. twice, 1 st. twice). 203—221 (171—187—187—203) sts. rem. Cont. in Mc., k. 1 row. Then work the shoulders. Allow 82—90 (70—76—76— 82) sts. at either side. P. 1 row on right side to form a stripe, work 5 rows st.st. for facing. Cast off shoulders and rem. sts. for neck.

SLEEVES:

Using set of needles no. 13 and Mc. cast on 64 sts., all sizes (54—60) sts. and work 1½ ins. in rib. Cont. in st.st. K. 1 rd., inc. 1 st. at end of same. Change to set of needles no. 10. x. Inc. 2 sts. at underarm, 1 st. either side of the first and last st. every 8th rd., working the extra sts. into patt., until there are 91— 93 (81—85—95—97) sts. Work in same border sequence and inc. likewise as for Two Needle Method. Having completed border III cont. in Mc., k. 1 rd., turn sleeve inside out and k. 6 rds. for seam facing. Cast off.

BUTTON BAND:

Using no. 13 needles and Mc. cast on 5 sts. for facing, pick up the sts. from Left Front. Cont. in rib but work the facing in st.st. When Band reaches neckline, cast off the 5 sts., place rem. sts. on a holder. Mark position of buttons, spacing evenly. Allow for one in neckband. 6—7 (5—6) in all. Work opposite Band to match making corresponding buttonholes as before.

TO MAKE UP:

Darn in all loose ends. Press. Measure width of sleeve tops and mark corresponding length on Jacket for armholes. Machine twice around same and down centre, to prevent fraying and cut between the machining. Join shoulders sewing through the p. stripe on right side. Slip st. around facings. Attach sleeves carefully matching centres to shoulders. Sew through the p. stripe and in chain of sts. just beyond the machining around armholes. Press seam, fold facing over raw edges on wrong side and slip st. Attach Front Bands. Fold facing over raw edges and slip st. Press well.

NECKBAND:

Using circular needle no. 13 work to and fro as for Two Needle Method. Complete as for Two Needle Method.

MAN'S AND BOY'S JACKET:

Using circular needle no. 13 and Mc. cast on 285—305—325—325 (225—245—245 —265) sts. and work 1 inch in k. 1, p. 1 rib, to and fro, fin. on wrong side. Next row: Rib to last 9 sts., cast off 5 sts. for buttonhole, rib to end. On next row cast on 5 sts. over those cast off. Complete the welt as for ladies Jacket. Cont. as for Lady's Jacket but allow 12 sts. for Front Bands. Cont. in border sequence as for Two Needle Method. On 50th (37th) rd. of border II shape the neck. Cast off the last 5—6—6—6 (4—4—4—5) sts. also the centre 3 sts. Next rd.: Cast off the first 5—6—6—6 (4—4—4—5) sts., k. to end. From here work to and fro, p. on wrong side. Further dec. at beg. of each row, all sizes, 3 sts. twice, 2 sts. once, 1 st. thrice (3—4—4—4 sts., then all sizes, 2 sts. twice, 1 st. twice). 221— 239—257—257 (171—187—187—203) sts. rem. Cont. in Mc. work 1 row. Then work the shoulders. Allow 90—98—106 —106 (70—76—76—82) sts. at both sides. P. 1 row on right side to form a stripe, work 5 rows st.st. for facing. Cast off shoulders and rem. sts. for neck.

SLEEVES:

Using set of needles no. 13 and Mc. cast on 72 sts. all sizes (54—60) sts. Work as for Lady's Sleeves to x. Inc. 2 sts. at underarm, 1 st. either side of the first and last st. every 8th rd. until there are 103—105 (81—85—95—97) sts. Cont. in same border sequence and inc. likewise as for Two Needle Method. Having completed border III cont. in Mc., k. 1 rd., turn sleeve inside out and k. 6 rds. for seam facing. Cast off.

TO MAKE UP:

As for Lady's Jacket.

NECKBAND:

Using circular needle no. 13 work to and fro as for Two Needle Method.

See page 44.

See page 36.

See page 30.

See page 42.

See page 40.

See page 29.

See page 54.

See page 14.

See page 12.

24

See page 16.

See page 39.

See page 6.

See page 52.

26

See page 32.

See page 34.

See page 4.

See page 8.

SHOWN IN COLOR ON PAGE 23.

LADY'S OR GIRL'S JUMPER

Size to fit 34-36-38 inch bust, 8-10-12-14 years.

Materials:

Size 34 36 38

	8	9	9	balls Red no. 681.
	7	8	9	« Grey no. 689.

8 10 12 14

5	5	6	7	balls White no. 501.
5	5	6	6	« Blue no. 707.

A pair of needles each no. 10 and 13 or 2 circular needles and set of needles each no. 10 and 13.

Actual measurements:

Size	34	36	38	8	10	12	14	
All round	35^1/$_2$	38^1/$_2$	41^1/$_2$	32	32	35^1/$_2$	35^1/$_2$	ins. approx.
Length	25	25	27	18^1/$_2$	20	21^1/$_2$	23^1/$_2$	« «
Sleeve seam	19	19^1/$_2$	20	14^1/$_2$	16	17	17^1/$_2$	« «

American		SIZE OF NEEDLES	0	3
British			13	10

TENSION:

26 stitches and 32 rows in pattern on no. 10 needles = 4 inches.
Check your tension very carefully. Adjust by using thicker or thinner needles.

ABBREVIATIONS:

Beg., beginning; cont., continue; fin., finishing; inc., increase; inc. 1 st., pick up loop between sts. and k. into back of same; k., knit; patt., pattern; p., purl; rem., remaining; rd., round; sts., stitches; st.st., stocking stitch; R., Red; W., White.

TWO NEEDLE METHOD

Girls sizes are in parentheses.

BACK AND FRONT ALIKE:

Using no. 13 needles and R. (W) cast on 119—129—139 (109—109—119—119) sts. and work 1^1/$_2$ ins. in k. 1, p. 1 rib, fin. on wrong side. Change to st.st., k. on right, p. on wrong side. Work 2 rows then change to no. 10 needles. x. Cont. in patt. from chart until entire work measures 24—24—26 (18^1/$_2$—20—21^1/$_2$—24) ins. 7—7—7^1/$_2$ (5—5^1/$_2$—6—6^1/$_2$) patts. Then using R. (W.) k. or p. 2 rows to form a stripe, work 6 (5) rows st.st. for facing. Cast off.

SLEEVES:

Using no. 13 needles and R. (W.) cast on 68 (58) sts. and work as Back to x. Inc. 1 st. at beg. of last row. Cont. in patt. and inc. 1 st. within the first and last st. every 8th row, working the extra sts. into patt., until there are 107—109—111 (81—85—93—95) sts. When entire sleeve measures 17^1/$_2$—18—18^1/$_2$ (13^1/$_2$—15—16—16^1/$_2$) ins. inc. likewise on every row 12 (10) times. 131—133—135 (101—105—113—115) sts. Then using R. (W.) p. or k. 2 rows to form a stripe. Cast off.

TO MAKE UP:

Darn in all loose ends. Omitting ribbing press work on wrong side with a hot iron over a damp cloth. Allow to dry. Join shoulders sewing through the p. stripe. Leave 9 (7^1/$_2$) ins. open for neck. Slip st. around facing. Join sides and sleeves, edge to edge flat seams. Attach sleeves carefully matching centres to shoulders. Sew through the p. stripe and in second chain of sts. on Jumper. Press all seams.

CIRCULAR KNITTING METHOD

BODY OF JUMPER:

Using circular needle no. 13 and R. (W.) cast on 250—260—270 (210—220—230—240) sts. and work 1^1/$_2$ ins. in k. 1, p. 1 rib. Change to st.st., k. all rds. K. 1 rd. then change to circular needle no. 10. x. Cont. in patt. from chart until entire work measures 24—24—26 (18^1/$_2$—20—21^1/$_2$—23^1/$_2$) ins. 7—7—7^1/$_2$ (5—5^1/$_2$—6—6^1/$_2$) patts. Then using R. (W.) k. 1 rd., p. 1 rd., k. 6 (5) rds. for facing. Cast off.

SLEEVES:

Using set of needles no. 13 and R. (W.) cast on 68 (58) sts. and work as Jumper to x. Inc. 1 st. at beg. of last rd. Cont. in patt. and inc. 2 sts. at underarm, 1 st. either side of the first and last st. every 8th rd., working the extra sts. into patt., until there are 107—109—111 (81—85—93—95) sts. When entire sleeve measures 17^1/$_2$—18—18^1/$_2$ (13^1/$_2$—15—16—16^1/$_2$) ins. inc. likewise on every rd. 12 (10) times. 131—133—135 (101—105—113—115) sts. Then using R. (W.) k. 1 rd., turn the work inside out and k. 6 (5) rds. for seam facing. Cast off.

TO MAKE UP:

Darn in all loose ends. Press. Measure width of sleeve tops and mark corresponding length on Jumper for armholes. Make sure that patts. match at armholes. Machine twice around same, to prevent fraying and cut between the machining. Join shoulders sewing through the p. stripe. Leave 9 (7^1/$_2$) ins. open for neck. carefully matching centres to shoulders. Sew through the p. stripe and in chain of sts. just beyond the machining around armholes.

Press seam, fold over raw edges on wrong side and slip st. to neaten. Press well.

☐ = Grey or Blue.   Begin all work here.
⊠ = Red or White.

SHOWN IN COLOR ON PAGE 22.

CHILD'S JUMPER

Size to fit 10—12—14 years

Materials:

Size 10 12 14

8 9 10 balls Red no. 140 or Light grey no. 2.
2 2 3 « Black no. 502 or White no. 501.
1 2 2 « Green no. 719 or Blue no. 671.
1 1 1 ball White no. 501 or Dark grey no. 689.

A pair of needles each no. 10 and 13 or 2 circular needles and set of needles each no. 10 and no. 13.

American		SIZE OF NEEDLES	0	3	
British				13	10
Actual chest measurement			30	32	34 ins.approx.
Length			19	21	23 « «
Sleeve seam			15	16	17 « «

TENSION:

26 stitches and 34 rows plain (30 rows pattern) on no. 10 needles = 4 inches.
Check your tension very carefully. Adjust by using thicker or thinner needles.

ABBREVIATIONS:

Beg., beginning; cont., continue; fin., finishing; inc., increase; inc. 1 st., pick up loop between sts. and k. into back of same; k., knit; patt., pattern; p., purl; rem., remaining; rep., repeat; rd., round; sts., stitches; st.st., stocking stitch; B., Black; Bl. Blue; Dg., Dark grey; G., Green; Lg., Light grey; R., Red; W., White.

TWO NEEDLE METHOD

BACK AND FRONT ALIKE:

Using no. 13 needles and G. or Dg. cast on 102—114—120 sts. and work 26 rows in k.2, p.2 rib as follows: 4 G. or Dg., 4 B. or Bl., 4 W., 4 R. or Lg., 6 B. or Dg., 4 G. or W. Then change to no. 10 needles and st.st. (k. on right, p. on wrong side). Inc. 1 st. at beg. of first row, all sizes. Cont. in main patt. from chart, work the first and last st. alike. When entire work measures 11½—12½ —13½ ins. shape the armholes: Cast off 3 sts. at beg. of next 2 rows then 1 st. at both ends of next 3 rows until 91—103—109 sts. rem. Cont. in main patt. until entire work measures 14—15½—17½ ins., fin. on a patt. row, then complete the border patt. Cont. in main patt. for 11 rows, then shape the shoulders: Cast off 23—27—29 sts. at beg. of next 2 rows and leave rem. sts. on a holder.

SLEEVES:

Using no. 13 needles and G. or Dg. cast on 54—60—60 sts. and work in rib as for Jumper. Change to no. 10 needles and st.st. Inc. 1 st. at beg. of first row, all sizes. Cont. in main patt. Further inc. 1 st. at both sides every 6th row, working the extra sts. into patt. until there are 79—91—91 sts. When entire sleeve measures 10—11½—12½ ins., fin. on a patt. row, complete the border patt. Inc. likewise to 85—97—97 sts. Cont. in main patt. Work 2 rows then inc. 1 st. at both sides of next 9 rows until there are 103—115—115 sts. Cast off.

TO MAKE UP:

Darn in all loose ends. Omitting ribbing press work on wrong side with a hot iron over a damp cloth. Allow to dry. Join sleeves, sides and right shoulder, edge to edge flat seams.
Collar: Using no. 13 needles pick up the sts. from holders and work in rib as for Jumper. Rep. these 26 rows. Cast off loosely. Join left shoulder and collar. Fold collar outwards. Attach sleeves carefully matching centres to shoulders. Press all seams.

CIRCULAR KNITTING METHOD

Using circular needle no. 13 and G. or Dg. cast on 216—228—240 sts. and work 26 rds. in k.2, p.2 rib as follows: 4 G. or Dg., 4 B. or Bl., 4 W., 4 R. or Lg., 6 B. or Dg., 4 G. or W. Change to circular needle no. 10 and st.st. (k. all rds.). Cont. in main patt. from chart until entire work measures 14—15½—17½ ins., fin. on a patt. rd., then complete the border patt. Cont. in main patt. for 11 rds. then shape the shoulders: Using R. or Lg. work the next 30—32—34 sts. thus: P.1 row on right side, 5 rows st.st. (k. on right, p. on wrong side) for facing. Cast off. Place the next 48—50—52 sts. on a holder for neck. Work the next 30—32—34 sts. as before. Rep. on rem. half of work.

SLEEVES:

Using set of needles no. 13 and G. or Dg. cast on 54—60—60 sts. and work in rib as for Jumper. Change to set of needles no. 10 st.st. Inc. 1 st. at beg. of first rd., all sizes. Cont. in main patt. Further inc. 2 sts. at underarm, 1 st. at either side of first and last st. of rd. every 6th rd. until there are 79—91—91 sts. When entire sleeve measures 10—11½—12½ ins., fin. on a patt. rd. complete the border patt. Inc. likewise to 85—97—97 sts. Cont. in main patt. K.2 rds. then inc. 1 st. at beg. and end of next 9 rds. until there are 103—115—115 sts. Finally turn work inside out and k.6 rds. in R. or Lg. for seam facing. Cast off.

TO MAKE UP:

Press. Measure width of sleeve tops and mark corresponding length on Jumper for armholes. Make sure that patts. match at armholes. Machine twice around armholes in chain of sts., to prevent fraying and cut between the machining. Fold shoulder facings on to wrong side and slip st. Join shoulders sewing through the p. stripe.
Collar: Using set of needles no. 13 (or small circular needle) pick up sts. from holders and work in rib as for Jumper. Rep. these 26 rds. Cast off loosely. Attach sleeves carefully matching centres to shoulder seams. Sew through the p. stripe and in chain of sts. just beyond the machining around armholes. Press seam, fold facing over raw edges on wrong side and slip st. to neaten. Press well.

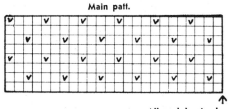

Border patt.

All work begins here

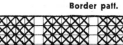

Main patt.

All work begins here

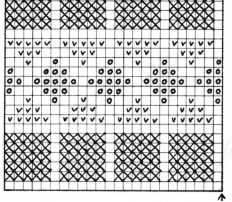

Border patt.

☐ = Red or Light grey
∨ = Black or Dark grey
✕ = Green or Blue
● = White

Main patt.

☐ = Red or Light grey
∨ = Black or White

SHOWN IN COLOR ON PAGE 27.

CHILD'S JUMPER, CAP, AND LEGGINGS

Jumper, size to fit 4—6—8—10 years

Leggings, size to fit 2—4 years

Materials:

Size	2	4	6	8	10	
Jumper		7	8	8	9	balls Marine no. 584 or White no. 501.
and Cap		2	2	2	3	« White no. 501 or Light blue no. 707.
Leggings	4	5				« Marine no. 584 or Light blue no. 707.

A pair of needles each no. 10 and no. 13 or 2 circular needles and set of needles each no. 10 and 13.

All round	......	24	26½	29	31½ ins.
Length	....	14½	16	18	19 ins.
Sleeve seam	...	10½	12	14	15 ins.

	SIZE OF NEEDLES	
American	0	3
British	13	10

LEGGINGS:

Waist	22	25	ins.
Hips	24½	27½	«
Length of back	10	11	«
Length of leg	13½	15	«

TENSION:

26 stitches and 34 rows plain (30 rows pattern) on no. 10 needles = 4 inches. **Check your tension very carefully. Adjust by using thicker or thinner needles.**

ABBREVIATIONS:

Beg., beginning; cont., continue, dec., decrease; fin., finishing; inc., increase; inc. l st., pick up loop between sts. and k. into back of same; k., knit; patt., pattern; p., purl; rem., remaining; rep., repeat; rd., round; sts., stitches; st. st., stocking stitch; tog., together; Mc., Main colour.

TWO NEEDLE METHOD

JUMPER

BACK AND FRONT ALIKE:

Using no. 13 needles and Mc. cast on 74—84—90—98 sts. and work 1½ ins. in k.1, p.1 rib, fin. on right side of work. Change to no. 10 needles. P.1 row whilst evenly inc. to 81—89—97—105 sts. Cont. in st. st. (k. on right, p. on wrong side) and main patt. from chart. Beg. as indicated, work the first and last st. alike. When entire work measures 9—10½—11½—12½ ins. shape the armholes: Cast off 3 sts. at beg. of next 2 rows then 1 st. at both ends of alternate rows twice, until 71—79—87—95 sts. rem. Cont. in main patt. until entire work measures 10½—12—13½—15 ins. approx., fin. after 8 plain rows. Then complete the border patt., beg. as indicated. Cast off.

SLEEVES:

Using no. 13 needles and Mc. cast on 42—44—46—48 sts. and work 2 ins. in rib as before, fin. on right side. Change to no. 10 needles. P.1 row whilst evenly inc. to 53—53—57—57 sts. Cont. in st. st. and main patt., beg. as indicated. Further inc. 1 st. at both sides every 6th row, working the extra sts. into patt., until there are 75—79—85—89 sts. Cont. until entire sleeve measures 10½—12—13½—15 ins., fin. on a suitable patt. row. Cast off.

TO MAKE UP:

Darn in all loose ends. Omitting ribbing press work on wrong side with a hot iron over a damp cloth. Allow to dry. Join sleeves, sides and right shoulder, edge to edge flat seams. Leave 7—8 ins. open for neck.

COLLAR:

Using no. 13 needles and Mc. pick up 100—104—108—112 sts. around neckline and work 3—4—4½—4½ ins. in rib as before. Cast off loosely ribwise. Join left shoulder and collar. Attach sleeves carefully matching centres to shoulder seams. Press all seams.

CAP

Using no. 13 needles and Mc. cast on 94—100—104—108 sts. and work 3 ins. in rib as before, fin. on right side of work. Change to no. 10 needles. P.1 row whilst evenly inc. to 97—113—113—113 sts. Cont. in st. st. Work 4 rows then complete the border patt. Cont. in Mc. until entire Cap measures 8½—9—9½—9½ ins. Finally k.2 sts. tog. throughout. Thread double wool through rem. sts.

TO MAKE UP:

Press. Join and press seam. Draw tog. at top and fasten well. Make a large pompon and attach to crown.

LEGGINGS

RIGHT SIDE:

Using no. 13 needles and Mc. cast on 73—83 sts. and work in st. st. After 8

Main patt.

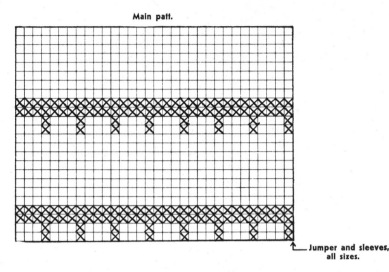

↑ Jumper and sleeves, all sizes.

☐ = Marine or White
✕ = White or Light blue

rows p.1 row on right side of work then work 8 rows more in st. st. Change to no. 10 needles. P.1 row.

Back shaping: K.14—16 sts., turn, p. to end. (Always slip the first st.). K.28—32 sts., turn, p. to end. Cont. likewise working 14—16 sts. more 3 times. Rep. over the 3 rem. sts. Cont on all sts. Then inc. 1 st. at same side as shaping every 10th—12th row, 5 times. But when work measures 9—10 ins. from p. stripe inc. 1 st. at opposite side also until there are 83—93 sts. Cont. without further shaping until entire work measures 10—11 ins. from p. stripe.
Leg: Dec. 1 st. at beg.of alternate rows, 9 times until 65—75 sts. rem. Work 2½—3 ins. without further shaping. Then dec. 1 st. at both sides of the centre 3 sts. every 6th row, 8—10 times until 49—55 sts. rem. Cont. without further shaping until leg measures 12—13½ ins. Finally work 1½ ins. in k.1, p.1 rib. Cast off.

LEFT SIDE:
As Right side but reverse shapings.

TO MAKE UP:
Press. Join legs and centre seams. Fold hem on to wrong side and slip st. Leave an opening for elastic. Thread in elastic to required waist measurement. Attach elastic to each ankle. Press all seams.

CIRCULAR KNITTING METHOD
JUMPER
BODY OF JUMPER:

Using circular needle no. 13 and Mc. cast on 150—166—182—198 sts. and work 1½ ins. in k.1, p.1 rib. Cont. in st. st. (k. all rds.). Inc. evenly on first rd. to 160—176—192—208 sts. Change to circular needle no. 10. Cont. in main patt. from chart until entire work measures 10½—12—13½—15 ins. approx., fin. after 8 plain rows. Then complete the border patt., beg. as indicated. Cast off.

SLEEVES:

Using set of needles no. 13 and Mc. cast on 42—44—46—48 sts. and work 2 ins. in rib as before. Cont. in st. st. Inc. evenly on first rd. to 53—53—57—57 sts. Change to set of needles no. 10. Cont. in main patt. Further inc. 2 sts. at underarm, 1 st. either side of the first and last st. of rd. every 6th rd., working the extra sts. into patt., until there are 75—79—85—89 sts. Cont. until entire sleeve measures 10½—12—13½—15 ins. fin. on a suitable patt. rd. Then turn work inside out and k.5 rds. in Mc. for seam facing. Cast off.

TO MAKE UP:

Press. Measure width of sleeve tops and mark corresponding length on Jumper for armholes. Make sure that patts. match at armholes. Machine twice around armholes in chain of sts., to prevent fraying, and cut between the machining. Join shoulders leaving 7—8 ins. open for neck. Attach sleeves

Border patt.

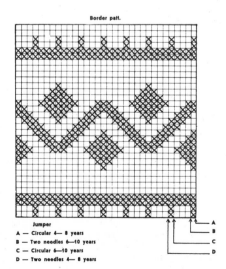

Jumper
A — Circular 4— 8 years
B — Two needles 6—10 years
C — Circular 6—10 years
D — Two needles 4— 8 years

A
B
C
D

carefully matching centres to shoulder seams. Sew through the p. stripe and in chain of sts. just beyond the machining around armholes. Press seam, fold facing over raw edges on wrong side and slip st. to neaten.

COLLAR:

Using set of needles no. 13 and Mc. pick up 100—104—108—112 sts. around neckline and work 3—4—4½—4½ ins. in rib as before. Cast off loosely ribwise.

CAP

Using set of needles no. 13 and Mc. cast on 94—100—104—108 sts. and work 3 ins. in rib as before. Cont. in st. st. Inc. evenly on first rd. to 96—112—112—112 sts. Change to set of needles no. 10. K.4 rds. then complete the border patt. Cont. in Mc. until entire Cap measures 8½—9—9½—9½ ins. Finally k.2 sts. tog. throughout. Thread double wool through rem. sts.

TO MAKE UP:

Press. Draw tog. at top and fasten well. Make a large pompon and attach to crown.

LEGGINGS

RIGHT SIDE:

Using circular needle no. 13 and Mc. cast on 146—166 sts. K.8 rds., p.1 rd., k.8 rds. Change to circular needle no. 10 and k.1 rd.

Back shaping: K. 14—16 sts., turn, p. to end. (Always slip the first st.). Rep. at opposite side. K. 28—32 sts., turn, p. to end. Rep. at opposite side. Cont. likewise working 14—16 sts. more each time until 6 sts. rem. at centre front. Turn, complete the rd. Cont. in st. st. Place a marking thread over the first and last st. of rd. and inc. 1 st. at either side of same every 10th—12th rd., 5 times. When work measures 9—10 ins. from p. stripe place a marking thread over the centre 2 sts. and inc. 1 st. at either side of same every alternate rd., 5 times. Cont. without further shaping until work measures 10—11 ins. from p. stripe.
Leg: Divide the work into two, 83—93 sts. Change to set of needles no. 10. K.2 sts. tog., place a marking thread here and dec. 1 st. at either side of same, 9 times until 64—74 sts. rem. K.2½—3 ins. without further shaping. Then dec. 1 st. at both sides of the 2 centre sts. every 6th rd. until 48—54 sts. rem. Cont. without further shaping until leg measures 12—13½ ins. Finally work 1½ ins. in k.1, p.1 rib. Cast off.

TO MAKE UP:

Press. Fold hem on to wrong side and slip st. Leave an opening for elastic. Thread in elastic to required waist measurement. Attach elastic to each ankle.

SHOWN IN COLOR ON PAGE 27.

LADY'S JUMPER AND CAP

Size to fit 34-36-37-38 inch bust.

Materials:

Size	34	36/37	38	
	12	13	14	balls White no. 501 or Black no. 502.
	4	4	5	« Black or White.

A pair of needles each no. 10 and 13 or 2 circular needles and set of needles no. 10.

Amercian	SIZE OF NEEDLES	0	3
British		13	10

TENSION:
26 stitches and 34 rows (30 rows in pattern) on no. 10 needles = 4 inches.
Check your tension very carefully. Adjust by using thicker or thinner needles.

ABBREVIATIONS:
Beg., beginning; cont., continue; dec., decrease; fin., finishing; inc., increase; inc. 1 st., pick up loop between sts. and k. into back of same; k., knit; patt., pattern; p., purl; rem., remaining; rep., repeat; rd., round; sts., stitches; st. st., stocking stitch; tog., together; Mc., Main colour.

TWO NEEDLE METHOD

BACK AND FRONT ALIKE:
Using no. 13 needles and Mc. cast on 120—125—130—135 sts. and work 1½

ins. in k. 1, p. 1 rib, fin. on wrong side. Change to no. 10 needles and st. st. (k. on right, p. on wrong side). When entire work measures 14—15—16—17 ins., fin. on wrong side, cast off 8 sts. at beg. of next 2 rows. Leave work aside.

SLEEVES:
Using no. 10 needles and Mc. cast on 55—55—61—61 sts. and work in st. st. After 6 rows for hem, p. 1 row on right side. Work 2 rows then complete the small border, from chart. Inc. 1 st. at end of last row. Cont. in Mc. Inc. 1 st. within the first and last st. every 6th row until there are 106—108—114—116 sts. When entire sleeve measures 17—17½—18—19 ins., fin. on wrong side, cast off 8 sts. at beg. of next 2 rows. Place rem. sts. on a holder.

YOKE: BACK AND FRONT ALIKE:
Using no. 10 needles pick up 45—46—49—50 sts. (beg. at centre) from one Sleeve, entire Back, 45—46—49—50 sts. from the other Sleeve (beg at edge). 194—201—212—219 sts. Work 6 rows. On third row dec. at regular intervals to 193—199—211—217 sts. Complete the border patt., from chart, dec. on first shaping thus: K. tog. the following sts. throughout. Two sets of figures denote the first and last two sizes.
Size 34: 31st and 32nd. 187 sts. rem.
Size 36 / 38: 15th and 16th, apart from the centre 7—9 sts. each side. 187—204 sts. rem.
Size 37: 29th and 30th. 204 sts. rem.
2nd—6th shaping: K. tog. the two sts. as indicated. 77—84 sts. rem.
7th shaping: 6th and 7th. 66—72 sts. rem.
8th shaping: 5th and 6th. 55—60 sts. rem.

Complete the chart. Cont. in Mc., work 1 row on right side to form a stripe, work 6 rows for facing. Cast off.

TO MAKE UP:

Darn in all loose ends. Omitting ribbing press work on wrong side with a hot iron over a damp cloth. Allow to dry. Join together, edge to edge flat seams. Fold neck facing and hem of sleeves on to wrong side and slip st. Press all seams.

CAP:

Using no. 13 needles and Mc. cast on 124 sts., all sizes. Work 4 ins. in rib as before, fin. on wrong side. Change to st. st., work 2 rows. Inc. on last row at regular intervals to 136 sts. Change to no. 10 needles. Cont. in patt. as indicated. Finally work 4 rows in Mc. Thread double wool through rem. sts.

TO MAKE UP:

Press. Join, press seam. Draw together at top and fasten well. Make a large pompon and attach to crown.

CIRCULAR KNITTING METHOD

BODY OF JUMPER:

Using circular needle no. 13 and Mc. cast on 240—250—260—270 sts. and work 1½ ins. in k. 1, p. 1 rib. Change to st. st. (k. all rds.). K. 1 rd. Change to circular needle no. 10. When entire work measures 14—15—16—17 ins. shape armholes. x Cast off 8, k. 104—109—114—119, cast off 8 sts. Place a marker here to denote side. x Rep. from x—x.

SLEEVES:

Using set of needles no. 10 and Mc. cast on 55—55—61—61 sts. and work in st. st. K. 6 rds., for hem, p. 1 rd., k. 2 rds. Then complete the small border. Cont. in Mc. Inc. 2 sts. at underarm, 1 st. at either side of the first and last st. every 6th rd. until there are 105—107—113—115 sts. When entire sleeve measures 17—17½—18—19 ins. shape the armhole. Cast off 8, k. 89—91—97—99, cast off 8 sts. Place on a holder.

YOKE:

Using circular needle no. 10 k. the sts. on to same as follows: 44—45—48—49 sts. from one Sleeve (beg. at centre), entire Back, Sleeve, Front and rem. 45—46—49—50 sts. from the other Sleeve.

K. 6 rds. On third rd. dec. at regular intervals to 384—396—420—432 sts. Complete the border patt. from chart, dec. on first shaping thus: (Two sets of figures denote the first and last two sizes.)
Size 34 / 37: K. 2 tog. at regular intervals 10—12 times. 374—408 sts. rem.
Size 35 / 38: K. tog. the 17th and 18th st. throughout. 374—408 sts. rem.
2nd—6th shaping: K. tog. the 2 sts. as indicated. 154—168 sts. rem.
7th shaping: 6th and 7th st. 132—144 sts. rem.
8th shaping: 5th and 6th st. 110—120 sts. rem.
Complete the chart. Cont. in Mc., k. 1 rd., p. 1 rd., k. 6 rds. for facing. Cast off.

TO MAKE UP:

Join at underarms. Otherwise as for Two Needle Method, apart from seams.

CAP:

Using set of needles no. 13 and Mc. cast on 124 sts., all sizes. Work 4 ins. in rib as before. K. 1 rd., inc. evenly on same to 136 sts. Change to set of needles no. 10. Cont. in patt. as indicated. Finally k. 4 rds. in Mc.

TO MAKE UP:

As for Two Needle Method, apart from seam.

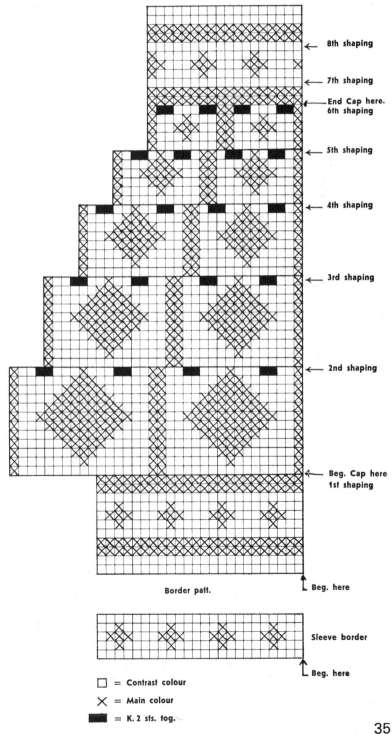

← 8th shaping

← 7th shaping

← End Cap here.
6th shaping

← 5th shaping

← 4th shaping

← 3rd shaping

← 2nd shaping

← Beg. Cap here.
1st shaping

← Beg. here

Border patt.

Sleeve border

Beg. here

□ = Contrast colour

✕ = Main colour

■ = K. 2 sts. tog.

SHOWN IN COLOR ON PAGE 21.

CHILD'S JUMPER, CAP, SCARF, MITTENS, AND LEGGINGS

Size to fit 4—6—8—10 years, Leggings 2—4 years

Materials:

Jumper and

Set. Size	2	4	6	8	10		
		6	7	8	9	balls	Blue no. 584 or Charcoal no. 12.
		2	3	3	3	«	Red no. 140 or Red no. 681.
		1	2	2	2	«	Mustard no. 748 or Green no. 733.
		1	1	2	2	«	Green no. 822 or White no. 17.
		1	1	1	1	ball	White no. 501 or Mustard no. 748.
Leggings		4	5			balls	Blue no. 584 or Charcoal no. 12.

A pair of needles each no. 10, 12, 13 or 3 circular needles, set of needles each no. 10, 12, 13 and a pair of needles each no. 10 and 12.

Actual measurements:

Size	4	6	8	10 years
Chest	26½	26½	29	31 ins.
Length	13	15	17	18 «
Sleeve seam	10	12	14	15 «

	SIZE OF NEEDLES		
American	0	1	3
British	13	12	10

TENSION:

26 stitches and 34 rows plain (30 rows pattern) on no. 10 needles = 4 inches. **Check your tension very carefully. Adjust by using thicker or thinner needles.**

ABBREVIATIONS:

Beg., beginning; cont., continue: dec., decrease; fin., finishing; inc., increase; inc. 1 st., pick up loop between sts. and k. into back of same; k., knit; patt., pattern; p., purl; rem., remaining; rep., repeat; rd., round; sts., stitches; st.st., stocking stitch; tog., together; G., Green; Mc., Main colour; M., Mustard; R., Red; W., White.

TWO NEEDLE METHOD

JUMPER

BACK:

Using no. 12 needles and Mc. cast on 89—89—97—105 sts. Work in st.st. throughout (k. on right, p. on wrong side). Work 5 rows, k.1 row on wrong side for hem, work 5 rows. Change to no. 10 needles, p.1 row. x Complete border I from chart, beg. as indicated, work the first and last st. alike. Cont. in Mc. as follows:

Size 4 and 6: Work 4 rows. Next row: (k.6, wool over needle, k.2 tog.) to end.

All sizes: Cont. until work measures 10—12—14—15 ins. from hem stripe, fin. on wrong side. Complete border II. Then k. the first and last 27—27—30—33 sts. and place on holder, cast off rem. 35—35—37—39 sts.

FRONT:

Work as for Back until work measures 8—10—12—13 ins. from hem stripe, fin. on wrong side. Then work each side separately:

LEFT SIDE:

K.39—39—43—46 sts. Cont. on same for 2—2—2—2 ins., fin. on wrong side. Complete border II but on 19th row shape neck: K.31—31—35—38 sts., turn, cast off 2 sts., p. to end. On following p. rows cast off 2—2—3—3 sts. at neck edge. Place the rem. 27—27—30—33 sts. on a holder.

RIGHT SIDE:

K. the first 5—5—5—6, cast off 1, k. the next 5—5—5—6 sts. and place on holders. Work the rem. sts. as Left Side reversing shaping. Make certain that patts. match at shoulders and centre.

SLEEVES:

Using no. 12 needles and Mc. cast on 47—51—53—55 sts. Work as for Jumper as far as x. Complete border I, beg. as indicated, but inc. 1 st. at both sides every 8th row. Cont. in Mc., inc. likewise until sleeve measures 8½—10½—12—13 ins from hem stripe. Then work 8—10—10—12 rows in R. 71—77—83—89 sts. Work 4—5—5—6 rows in G., inc. likewise on each row. 79—87—93—101 sts. Finally p.1 row, k.1 row both on right side. Cast off.

TO MAKE UP:

Darn in all loose ends. Omitting ribbing press work on wrong side with a hot iron over a damp cloth. Allow to dry. Join sides and sleeves, edge to edge flat seams. Graft shoulders. Attach sleeves carefully matching centres to shoulders. Sew through the p. stripe and in second chain of sts. on Jumper. Slip st. around hems.

NECKBAND:

Using no. 10 needles and R. pick up the 5—5—5—6 sts. from Left front, right side facing. Cast on 6—6—6—7 sts. at centre and 1 st. at opposite side. Cont. in st.st. but slip the 7th—7th—7th—8th st. on k. rows. The band is folded here. When the band reaches around neckline (allow for mitres) cast off the extra st. at side, graft the next 5—5—5—6 sts. to front of Jumper, cast off rem. Attach to neckline, press seam and slip st. around facing on wrong side. Press all seams. Attach buttons, make corresponding loops.

Size 4 and 6: Twist a cord and thread through holes at waist. Make 2 pompons and attach to each end.

CAP:

Using no. 12 needles and Mc. cast on 121—129 sts. and work 1 inch in k.1, p.1 rib, fin. on wrong side. Change to no. 10 needles and st.st. Work 2 rows, complete border I. Cont. in Mc., work 2 rows then 2½—3½ ins. in k.1, p.1 rib, fin on wrong side. Next row: K.3 sts. tog. throughout. P.1 row. Thread double wool through sts. Press. Join and press seam. Draw together and fasten well. Make a multi-coloured pompon and attach to crown.

EAR MUFFS: (Both alike)

Using no. 12 needles and Mc. cast on 28—32 sts. and work 2—2½ ins. in k.1, p.1 rib. Then dec. 1 st. at both sides on alternate rows until 12—14 sts. rem. Cont. for 6 ins. Cast off. Attach to inside of Cap.

SCARF:

Using no. 10 needles and R. cast on 170—186—200—210 sts. Work in st.st. Work 4 rows, p.1 row on right side, 8—10—10—12 rows more. Then 4—5—5—6 in G., 2 in W. or M., 2 in M. or W. Rep. in reverse order. Press. Fold on p. stripes, join seam. Press well. Attach fringe to ends.

MITTENS:

Using no. 13 needles and Mc. cast on 38—42—46—46 sts. and work 2—2—2½—2½ ins. in k.1, p.1 rib, fin on wrong side. K.1 row. Change to no. 10 needles and st.st. Work the first 6 rows of border II, upside down. Cont. in Mc., p.1 row.

Right mitten: K.2 sts., place a marking thread here, inc. 1, k.1 st., inc. 1, place another marker here, k. to end. Cont. to inc. 1 st. within each marker on every k.

row until there are 3—5—5—5 sts. between same. P.1 row.

Next row: K.1 st., place the next 5—7—7—7 sts. on a holder, cast on 5—7—7—7 sts., k. to end. Cont. until entire work measures 4½—5—5½—5½ ins., fin. on wrong side.

Shaping: K.20—23—25—25 sts., turn, dec. 1 st. within the first and last st. until 4—5—5—5 sts. rem. Thread wool through sts. Rep. on rem. sts.

Thumb: Pick up the sts. from holder, 1 st. at each side and 5—7—7—7 sts. opposite, where cast on. In all 12—16—16—16 sts. Work 1—1½—2—2 ins in st.st. Then divide the sts. equally and shape as for mitten.

Border II

Jumper and Cap.

Border I.

Jumper and Cap.
Sleeves, size 4.
Sleeves, size 10.
Sleeves, size 8.
Sleeves, size 6.

☐ = Blue or Charcoal.
✕ = White or Mustard.
● = Green or White
∨ = Red
■ = Mustard or Green.

LEFT MITTEN:

Work as for Right Mitten but k.16—18—20—20 instead of 2 sts. before inc. for Thumb.

Press. Join together. Press all seams.

LEGGINGS

Waist	22	25	ins.
Hips	24½	27½	«
Length of Back	10	11	«
Length of Leg	13½	15	«

LEGGINGS
RIGHT SIDE:

Using no. 13 needles and Mc. cast on 73—83 sts. and work in st.st. After 8 rows p.1 row on right side then work 8 rows more in st.st. Change to no. 10 needles. P.1 row.

Back shaping: K. 14—16 sts., turn, p. to end. (Always slip the first st.). K.28—32 sts., turn, p. to end. Cont. likewise working 14—16 sts. more 3 times. Rep. over the 3 rem. sts. Cont. on all sts. Then inc. 1 st. at same side as shaping every 10th—12th row, 5 times. But when work measures 9—10 ins. from p. stripe inc. 1 st. at opposite side also until there are 83—93 sts. Cont. without further shaping until entire work measures 10—11 ins. from p. stripe.

Leg: Dec. 1 st. at beg. of alternate rows 9 times until 65—75 sts. rem. Work 2½—3 ins. without further shaping. Then dec. 1 st. at both sides of the centre 3 sts. every 6th row 8—10 times until 49—55 sts. rem. Cont. without further shaping until leg measures 12—13½ ins. Finally work 1½ ins. in k.1, p.1 rib. Cast off.

LEFT SIDE:

As Right Side but reverse shapings.

TO MAKE UP:

Press. Join legs and centre seams. Fold hem on to wrong side and slip st. Leave an opening for elastic. Thread in elastic to required waist measurement. Attach elastic to each ankle. Press all seams.

CIRCULAR KNITTING METHOD

BODY OF JUMPER:

Using circular needle no. 12 and Mc. cast on 176—176—192—208 sts. Work in st.st. (k. all rds.) throughout. K.5 rds., p.1 rd. for hem, k.5 rds. Change to circular needle no. 10 and k.1 rd. x Then complete border 1 from chart, beg. as indicated. Cont. in Mc. as follows:

Size 4 and 6: K.4 rds. Next rd.: (K.6, wool over needle, k.2 tog.) to end.

All sizes: Cont. until work measures 8—10—12—13 ins. from p. stripe. Next rd.: Divide sts. for Front: K.39—39—43—46, place the next 10—10—10—12 sts. on a holder. Cast on 4 sts. (the work is cut here later) and work these in plain colour throughout. K.39—39—43—46 sts., place a marking thread here to denote side, k. to end of rd. There should now be 170—170—186—200 sts. Cont. until work measures 10—12—14—15 ins. from p. stripe. Then complete border II as follows: K.39—39—43—46 sts. in patt., k. the extra 4 sts. in plain colour, k. the next 39—39—43—46 sts. in patt. to correspond. Make sure that design matches at centres and sides.

N.B. Beg. patt. on Back at same place as on Front. Inc. 1 st. on Back. On 19th patt. rd. shape neck: Change to a pair of no. 10 needles and work to and fro (k. on right, p. on wrong side).
Left side: Cont. in patt., k. the first 31—31—35—38 sts., turn, cast off 2 sts., p. to end. On following p. rows cast off 2—2—3—3 sts. at neck edge. Leave the rem. 27—27—30—33 sts. on holders for shoulders.
Right side: Cast off the next 20 sts. for neck, work the rem. 31—31—35—38 sts. as Left Side, reversing shaping.
Back: Complete border II. Place the first and last 27—27—30—33 sts. on holder, cast off rem. 35—35—37—39 sts.

SLEEVES:

Using set of needles no. 12 and Mc. cast on 46—50—52—54 sts. Work as for Jumper to x. Inc. 1 st. on last rd. Complete border I, beg. as indicated, but inc. 2 sts. at underarm, 1 st. either side of the first and last st. of rd. every 6th rd. Cont. in Mc. inc. likewise until sleeve measures 8½—10½—12—13 ins. from p. stripe. Then k.8—10—10—12 rds. in R. 71—77—83—89 sts. K.4—5—5—6 rds. in G. and inc. likewise on each rd. 79—87—93—101 sts. Finally p.1 rd., k.4 rds. for seam facing. Cast off.

TO MAKE UP:

Darn in all loose ends. Press. Graft shoulders. Measure width of sleeve tops and mark corresponding length on Jumper for armholes. Machine twice around armholes and cut between the machining. Attach sleeves carefully matching centres to shoulders. Sew through the p. stripe and in chain of sts. just beyond the machining around armholes. Press seam, fold facing over raw edges on wrong side and slip st. to neaten.

NECKBAND:

Using a pair of needles no. 10 and R. pick up the 5—5—5—6 sts. from Left Front, right side facing and cast on 8—8—8—9 sts. at centre, 1 st. at opposite edge. Cont. in st.st. but slip the 9th—9th—9th—10th st. on k. rows. The band is folded here. When the band reaches around neckline (allow for mitres) cast off the extra st. at side, graft the next 5—5—5—6 sts. to front of Jumper, cast off the rem. sts. Machine twice down the centre 4 sts. and cut between the machining. Attach neckband, press seam, fold facing over raw edges on wrong side and slip st. to neaten. Slip st. around hems. Press well. Attach buttons and make corresponding loops.
Size 4 and 6: Twist a cord and thread through holes at waist. Make two pompons and attach to each end.

CAP:

Using set of needles no. 12 and Mc. cast on 120—128 sts. and work 1 inch in k.1, p.1 rib. Change to set of needles no. 10 and st.st. K.2 rds. Complete border I. Cont. in Mc., k. 2 rds. then work 2½—3½ ins. in k.1, p.1 rib. Next rd: K.3 sts. tog. throughout. Thread double wool through rem. sts. Press. Draw together and fasten well. Make a multi-coloured pompon and attach to crown.

EAR MUFFS:

As for Two Needle Method.

SCARF:

As for Two Needle Method.

MITTENS:

Using set of needles no. 13 and Mc. cast on 38—42—46—46 sts. and work 2—2—2½—2½ ins. in k.1, p.1 rib. K.1 rd. Change to set of needles no. 10. Cont. in st.st. K. the first 6 rds. of border II, upside down. Cont. in Mc., k.1 rd.
Right mitten: K.2 sts., place a marking thread here, inc. 1, k.1, inc. 1 st., place another marker here, k. to end of rd. K.1 rd. without shaping. Cont. to inc. 1 st. within each marker on alternate rds. until there are 3—5—5—5 sts. between same. K.1 rd.
Next rd.: K.1 st. place the next 5—7—7—7 sts. on a holder, cast on 5—7—7—7 sts., k. to end of rd. Cont. until entire work measures 4½—5—5½—5½ ins. Then divide the sts. equally and place a marker at each side.
Shaping: x K.1, slip 1, k.1, pass the slip st. over, k. to the last 3 sts. before next marker, k.2 tog., k.1 st. x Rep. from x—x. Dec. likewise until 6 sts. rem. Thread wool through sts. and draw together.
Left Mitten: As for Right Mitten but k.16—18—20—20 sts. instead of 2 sts. before inc. for Thumb.

THUMB:

Pick up the sts. from holder, 1 st. at each side and 5—7—7—7 sts. where sts. were cast on. K.1—1½—2—2 ins. Then divide the sts. equally and shape as for mitten. Draw together. Press well.

LEGGINGS
RIGHT SIDE:

Using circular needle no. 13 and Mc. cast on 146—166 sts. K.8 rds., p.1 rd., k.8 rds. Change to circular needle no. 10 and k.1 rd.
Back Shaping: K.14—16 sts., turn, (always slip the first st.) p. back. Rep. at opposite side. Cont. likewise working 14—16 sts. more each time until 6 sts. rem. at centre front. Turn, complete the rd. Cont. in st.st. Place a marking thread over the first and last st. of rd. and inc. 1 st. at either side of same every 10th—12th rd., 5 times. When work measures 9—10 ins. from p. stripe place a marking thread over the centre 2 sts. and inc. 1 st. at either side of same every alternate rd., 5 times. Cont. without further shaping until work measures 10—11 ins. from p. stripe.
Shape Leg: Divide the work into two, 83—93 sts. Change to set of needles no. 10. K.2 tog., place a marker here and dec. 1 st. at either side of same 9 times until 64—74 sts. rem. Cont. without further shaping for 2½—3 ins. Then dec. 1 st. at both sides of the centre 2 sts. every 6th rd. until 48—54 sts. rem. Cont. without further shaping until leg measures 12—13½ ins. Finally work 1½ ins. in k.1, p. 1 rib. Cast off.

TO MAKE UP:

Press. Attach elastic as for Two Needle Method.

SHOWN IN COLOR ON PAGE 25.

LADY'S JUMPER

Size to fit 34—36—38 inch bust

Materials:

Size 34 36 38
12 13 14 balls Blue no. 707.
2 3 3 balls White no. 501.

A pair of needles each no. 10, 12 and 13 or 2 circular needles each no. 10 and 13 and 2 sets of needles each no. 10 and 12.

Actual measurements:

All round	36 —38	/ 38 —40 ins.
Length	24½—25	/ 26 —27 ins.
Sleeve seam	19 —19½	/ 19½—20 ins.

American		SIZE OF NEEDLES	0	1	3
British			13	12	10

TENSION:

26 stitches and 34 rows in main pattern on no. 10 needles = 4 inches. **Check your tension very carefully. Adjust by using thicker or thinner needles.**

ABBREVIATIONS:

Beg., beginning; cont., continue; fin., finishing; inc., increase; inc., 1 st., pick up loop between sts. and k. into back of same; k., knit; patt., pattern; p., purl; rem., remaining; rep., repeat; rd., round; sts., stitches; st.st., stocking stitch; B., Blue; W., White.

TWO NEEDLE METHOD

BACK AND FRONT ALIKE:

Using no. 13 needles and W. cast on 113—121 / 121—129 sts. Work 14 rows in st.st. (k. on right, p. on wrong side), p. 1 row on right side for hem. Change to no. 10 needles and work 14 rows st.st. Then complete the border patt. from chart. Cont. in B. only and main patt. as follows:

1st row: K. on right side.
2nd row: x K.1, p.7, x Rep. from x—x to last st., k.1.
Rep. these 2 rows throughout. Inc. 1 st. at both sides, within the first and last st., every 20th row 4 times until there are 121—129 / 129—137 sts. Cont. until

work measures 21½—22 / 22½—23½ ins. from p.stripe. Then complete the border patt. upside down, in line with the lower border. Cont. in W., work 14 rows st.st., p.1 row on right side and 14 rows st.st. for facing. Cast off.

SLEEVES:

Using no. 12 needles and B. cast on 57—57 / 65—65 sts. Work 2½ ins. in k.1, p.1 rib, fin. on wrong side. Change to no. 10 needles. Cont. in main patt. but inc. 1 st. at both sides every 6th row, working the extra sts. into patt., until there are 103—105 / 109—111 sts. Cont. until entire sleeve measures 17—17½ / 18—18½ ins. then inc. likewise on the next 12 rows, 127—129 / 133—135 sts. Finally k.1 row, p.1 row both on right side of work. Cast off.

TO MAKE UP:

Darn in all loose ends. Press work on wrong side with a hot iron over a damp cloth. Allow to dry. Join sides and sleeves, edge to edge flat seams. Slip st. around hem and facing. Join shoulders leaving 9 ins. open for neck. Sew through the p.loops on right side of work. Attach sleeves carefully matching centres to shoulders. Sew through

the p. stripe and in second chain of sts. on Jumper. Press all seams.

CIRCULAR KNITTING METHOD

BODY OF JUMPER:

Using circular needle no. 13 and W. cast on 224—240 / 240—256 sts. K.14 rds., p.1 rd. for hem. Change to circular needle no. 10 and k.14 rds. Then complete border patt. from chart. Place a marking thread at beg. of rd. and one after 112—120 / 120—128 sts. to denote sides. Cont. in B. only and main patt. as follows:
1st rd: K.
2nd rd.: x P.1, k.7, x Rep. from x—x to end. Rep. these 2 rds. throughout. Inc. 1 st. either side of markers (4 in all) every 20th rd. 4 times until there are 240—256 / 256—272 sts. Cont. until work measures 21½—22 / 22½—23½ ins. from p.stripe. Then complete the border patt. upside down, in line with the lower border. Cont. in W., k.14 rds., p.1 rd., k.14 rds. for facing. Cast off.

SLEEVES:

Using set of needles no. 12 and B. cast on 56—56 / 64—64 sts. and work 2½ ins. in k.1, p.1 rib. K.1 rd., inc. 1 st. at end of same. Change to set of needles no. 10. Cont. in main patt. but inc. 2 sts. at underarm. 1 st. either side of the first and last st. of rd. every 6th rd. until there are 103—105 / 109—111 sts. Cont. until entire sleeve measures 17—17½ / 18—18½ ins. then inc. likewise on the next 12 rds., 127—129 / 133—135 sts. Finally k.1 rd., p.6 rds. for seam facing. Cast off.

TO MAKE UP:

Darn in all loose ends. Press. Slip st. around hem and facing. Join shoulders sewing through p.loops on right side of work. Leave 9 ins. open for neck. Measure width of sleeve tops and mark corresponding length on Jumper for armholes. Make sure that patts. are alike at each side. Machine twice around armholes, to prevent fraying and cut between the machining. Attach sleeves carefully matching centres to shoulders. Sew through the first p.rd. and in chain of sts. just beyond the machining around armholes. Press seam, fold facing over raw edges on wrong side and slip st. to neaten. Press well.

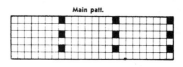

Main patt.

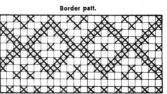

Border patt.

Beg. here.

□ = Blue.
✕ = White.
■ = P.st. on right side.

SHOWN IN COLOR ON PAGE 23.

MAN'S JACKET

Size to fit 38—40—42—44 inch chest

Materials:

Size	38	40	42	44	
	9	10	11	12	balls Light grey no. 5.
	6	7	7	8	« Dark grey no. 9.
	2	3	3	4	« White no. 501.
	1	1	1	1	ball Grey no. 689.

A pair of needles each no. 10 and 13 or circular needles and set of needles each no. 10 and 13.

American		SIZE OF NEEDLES 0 3
British		13 10

Actual measurements:

Size	38	40	42	44	
All round	41	43	45	47	ins. approx.
Length	27	27½	28	29	« «
Sleeve seam	20½	20½	21	21½	« «

TENSION:

26 stitches and 34 rows plain (30 rows pattern) on no. 10 needles = 4 inches.

Check your tension very carefully. Adjust by using thicker or thinner needles.

ABBREVIATIONS:

Beg., beginning; cont., continue; dec., decrease; fin., finishing; inc., increase; inc. 1 st., pick up loop between sts. and k. into back of same; k., knit; patt., pattern; p., purl; rem., remaining; rep., repeat; rd., round; sts., stitches; st. st., stocking stitch; tog., together; Dg., Dark grey; Lg., Light grey.

TWO NEEDLE METHOD

BACK:

Using no. 13 needles and Dg. cast on 133—141—145—153 sts. work 1½ ins. in k. 1, p. 1 rib, fin. on right side. P. 1 row. Change to no. 10 needles and st. st. (k. on right, p. on wrong side). Complete border I, from chart, beg. as indicated. Cont. in main patt. until entire work measures 23—23½—24½—25 ins., fin. with 3 rows in Lg. Complete border II, beg. as indicated. Then shape the shoulders. Cont. in Dg., work the first 44—47—48—51 sts., turn, p. 1 row on right side (k. on wrong side), cast off. Cast off next 45—47 / 49—51 sts. for neck.

RIGHT FRONT:

Using no. 13 needles and Dg. cast on 79—83—85—89 sts. and work the welt as before. P. 67—71—73—77 sts., inc. 1 st. for seam (work this in plain colour throughout) and leave rem. 12 sts. on a holder for Front Band. Change to no. 10 needles and st. st. Complete border I, beg. as indicated. Cont. in main patt. to match Back. Size 38 and 40: Dec. 1 st. at both sides before beg. same, inc. 1 st. at both sides for border II. Work the first 14 rows of border II then shape neck. Keeping continuity of patt. cast off the seam st. then 6—6—6—7 sts. Further dec. at beg. of k. rows 4—4—5—5, 3—4—4—4 sts. Then for all sizes 3 sts. once, 2 sts. thrice and finally 1 st. 44—47—48—51 sts. Cont. in Dg., k. 2 rows beg. on right side (p. on wrong side). Cast off.

LEFT FRONT:

Work as Right Front for 1 inch, fin. on right side. Next row: Rib 4, cast off 5 sts. for buttonhole, rib to end. On next row cast on 5 sts. over those cast off. Complete the welt, fin. on wrong side. K. 67—71—73—77 sts., inc. 1 st. for seam, leave the rem. 12 sts. on a holder. Cont. to match Right Front. Beg. patt. and neck shaping on p. rows.

SLEEVES:

Using no. 13 needles and Dg. cast on 71 sts. and work 2 ins. in rib as before, fin. on right side. P. 1 row. Change to no. 10 needles and st. st. Complete border I, beg. as indicated whilst inc. 1 st. at both sides on every 8th row 5 times. 81 sts. Cont. in main patt., inc. likewise on every 6th row. 115—117—119—121 sts. When entire sleeve measures 16½—17—17½—18 ins., fin. with 3 rows in Lg. work the first 19 rows of border II, inc. likewise. 123—125—127—129 sts. Then complete the patt., inc. likewise on every row. 147—149—151—153 sts. Cont. in Dg., k. 1, p. 1, k. 1 row on right side (p. 1, k. 1, p. 1 row on wrong side). Cast off.

BUTTON BAND:

Using no. 13 needles and Dg. pick up the sts. from Right Front, inc. 1 st. at inner edge for seam. Cont. in rib until band reaches to neckline, when slightly stretched. Cast off the seam st. and leave rem. sts. on a holder. Mark position of buttons, spacing evenly, allow for one in neckband. (6 in all.)

BUTTONHOLE BAND:

Work to match making corresponding buttonholes as before.

TO MAKE UP:

Darn in all loose ends. Omitting ribbing press work on wrong side with a hot iron over a damp cloth. Allow to dry. Join shoulders sewing through the p. stripe. Join sides and sleeves, edge to edge flat seams. Attach bands to fronts. Attach sleeves carefully matching centres to shoulders. Sew through the p. stripe and in second chain of sts. on Jacket.

NECKBAND:

Using no. 13 needles and Dg. pick up 137—139—141—143 sts. around neckline, right side facing, and work 2½ ins. in rib as before. Make a buttonhole after ½ inch and again after 1¾ ins. Cast off ribwise. Fold on to wrong side and slip st. Sew around buttonholes. Attach buttons. Press all seams.

CIRCULAR KNITTING METHOD

BODY OF JACKET:

Using circular needle no. 13 and Dg. cast on 295—305—315—325 sts. and work 1 inch in k. 1, p. 1 rib, to and fro, fin. on right side. Next row: Rib 4, cast off 5 sts., rib to end. On next row cast on 5 sts. over those cast off. Cont. in rib until work measures 1½ ins., fin. on wrong side. Next row: Rib 12 sts., place on a holder, k. to last 12 sts., place on a holder. Change to circular needle no. 10 and st. st. (k. all rds.). Cast on 3 sts. and join work into a rd., work these sts. in plain colour throughout. The work is cut here later. Complete border I, cont. in main patt. Size 38 and 42: Dec. 2 sts., 1 st. at either side of the centre 3 sts. before beg. same. Then inc. 1 st. likewise for border II. When entire work measures 23—23½—24—25½ ins., fin. with 3 rds. in Lg. work the first 14 rds. of border II. Then shape the neck. Next rd: Cont. in patt. to the last 6—6—6—7 sts. and cast them off. From here work to and fro, p. on wrong side. Cast off the centre 3 sts., then 6—6—6—7 sts., k. to end. Further dec. at beg. of each row 4—4—4—4, 3—4—4—4, 2—3—3—3 sts. Then for all sizes 2 sts. twice, 1 st. twice. Then work each shoulder separately. Allow 46—47—49—51 sts. for each. Using Dg. k. 2 rows, beg. on right side (p. on wrong side), work 5 rows st. st. for facing. Cast off. Cast off rem. sts. for neck.

SLEEVES:

Using set of needles no. 13 and Dg. cast on 70 sts. and work 2 ins. in rib as before. K. 1 rd. and inc. 1 st. on same. Change to set of needles no. 10. Complete border I whilst inc. 2 sts. at underarm, 1 st. at either side of the first and last st. of rds. every 8th rd. 5 times. 81 sts. Cont. in main patt., inc. likewise every 6th rd. 115—117—119—121 sts. When entire sleeve measures 16½—17—17½—18 ins., fin. with 3 rds. in Lg. work the first 19 rds. of border II, inc. likewise. 123—125—127—129 sts. Then complete the patt., inc. likewise on every rd. 147—149—151—153 sts. Cont. in Dg., k. 1 rd. Turn the work inside out, k. 6 rds. for facing. Cast off.

BUTTON BAND:

Using no. 13 needles and Dg. cast on 5 sts. for facing then pick up the 12 sts., right side facing, from Right front. Cont. in rib but work the facing in st. st. until band reaches to neckline. Then cast off the 5 sts. and leave rem. sts. on a holder. Mark position of buttons, spacing evenly, allow for one in neckband. (6 in all.)

BUTTONHOLE BAND:

Work to match making corresponding buttonholes as before.

TO MAKE UP:

Darn in all loose ends. Press. Measure width of sleeve tops and mark corresponding length on Jacket for armholes. Machine twice around armholes and down centre front, to prevent fraying, and cut between the machining. Fold shoulder facing on to wrong side and slip st. Join shoulders sewing through the p. stripes. Attach sleeves carefully matching centres to shoulders. Sew through the p. stripe and in chain of sts. just beyond the machining around armholes. Press seam, fold facing over raw edges on wrong side and slip st. to neaten. Attach bands to Fronts. Neaten likewise.

NECKBAND:

As for Two Needle Method. Press well. Attach buttons.

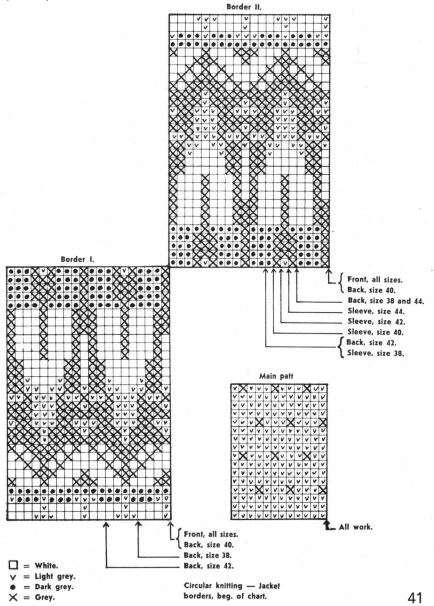

Border II.

Border I.

{ Front, all sizes.
{ Back, size 40.
— Back, size 38 and 44.
— Sleeve, size 44.
— Sleeve, size 42.
— Sleeve, size 40.
{ Back, size 42.
{ Sleeve, size 38.

Main patt

All work.

{ Front, all sizes.
— Back, size 40.
— Back, size 38.
— Back, size 42.

☐ = White.
v = Light grey.
● = Dark grey.
✕ = Grey.

Circular knitting — Jacket borders, beg. of chart.

41

SHOWN IN COLOR ON PAGE 22.

LADY'S JUMPER AND CAP

Size to fit 32—34—36—38 inch bust.

Materials:

Size 32 34 36 38
    13 14 14 14 balls White no. 501
      5   5   6   6 «   Mustard no. 764 or Dark green no. 734.
      2   3   3   3 «   Dark brown no. 581 or Light green no. 733.

A pair of needles each no. 10 and no. 13 or 2 circular needles and set of needles each no. 10 and 13.

Actual measurements:

		32	34	36	38	
All round	....	36	36	40	40	ins.
Length	....	24½	25	26	27	ins.
Sleeve seam	......	19	19½	20	20	ins.

	SIZE OF NEEDLES		
American		0	3
British		13	10

TENSION:

26 stitches and 34 rows plain (30 rows pattern) on no. 10 needles = 4 inches. **Check your tension very carefully. Adjust by using thicker or thinner needles.**

ABBREVIATIONS:

Beg., beginning; cont., continue; tin., finishing; inc., increase; inc. 1 st., pick up loop between sts. and k. into back of same; k., knit; patt., pattern; p., purl; rem., remaining; rd., round; sts., stitches; st.st., stocking stitch; tog., together; Dg., Dark green; M. Mustard; W., White.

TWO NEEDLE METHOD

BACK AND FRONT ALIKE:

Using no. 13 needles and M. or Dg. cast on 120—120—132—132 sts. and work in k.1, p.1 rib. After 2 rows work 1 inch in W., fin. on wrong side. Change to no. 10 needles and st.st. (k. on right, p. on wrong side). Size 32—34: Inc. 1 st. at beg. of first row. Cont. in patt. from chart. Complete border I, cont. in main patt. until entire work measures 15—16—16½—17½ ins. Then shape the shoulders: Cast off 3 sts. at beg. of next 2 rows then 1 st. twice until 111—111—112—112 sts. rem. Cont. until entire work measures 21—22—23—24 ins., fin. on a patt. row. Then complete border II, beg. as indicated. Cont. in M. or Dg., p.1 row on right side of work, 5 rows st.st. for facing. Cast off.

SLEEVES:

Using no. 13 needles and M. or Dg. cast on 58—60—62—64 sts. and work 1½ ins. in rib as before. Change to no. 10 needles and st.st. Inc. evenly on first row to 66 sts., all sizes. Further inc. 1 st. at both sides every 6th row, working the extra sts. into patt. Complete border I, 76 sts., cont. in main patt., inc. likewise to 104—104—106—106 sts. When entire sleeve measures 15½—16—16½—17 ins., fin. on a patt. row, complete border II. Beg as indicated. Inc. likewise 3 times, 110—110—112—112 sts. Finally inc. 1 st. at both sides of the last 10 rows, 130—130—132—132 sts. Cast off.

TO MAKE UP:

Darn in all loose ends. Omitting ribbing press work on wrong side with a hot iron over a damp cloth. Allow to dry. Fold facing at top on to wrong side and slip st. Join shoulders sewing through p.stripe. Leave 9 ins. open for neck. Join sleeves and sides, edge to edge flat seams. Attach sleeves carefully matching centres to shoulder seams.

COLLAR:

Using no. 13 needles and W. cast on 120—120—124—124 sts. and work 6½ ins. in rib as before. Cast off loosely ribwise. Join seam. Attach cast off edge to lower edge of collar. Fold collar outwards. Press all seams.

CAP:

Using no. 13 needles and M. or Dg. cast on 110 sts., all sizes, and work in rib as for Jumper. Change to no. 10 needles and st.st. Inc. evenly on first row to 121 sts. Complete border I, cont. in main patt. until entire Cap measures 9½ ins. Next row: K.2 sts. tog. throughout. Thread double wool through rem. sts.

TO MAKE UP:

Press. Join and press seam. Draw tog. at top and fasten well. Make a large pompon and attach to crown.

CIRCULAR KNITTING METHOD

BODY OF JUMPER:

Using circular needle no. 13 and M. or Dg. cast on 242—242—264—264 sts. and work in k.1, p.1 rib. After 2 rds. work 1 inch in W. Change to circular needle no. 10 and st.st. (k. all rds.). Complete border I, cont. in main patt. until entire work measures 15—16—16½—17½ ins., fin. on a patt. rd. Then complete border II. Cont. in M. or Dg., p.1 rd., k.5 rds for facing. Cast off.

SLEEVES:

Using set of needles no. 13 and M. or Dg. cast on 58—60—62—64 sts. and work 1½ ins. in rib as before. Change to set of needles no. 10 and st.st. Inc. evenly on first rd. to 66 sts., all sizes. Further inc. 2 sts. at underarm, 1 st. either side of the first and last st. of rd., working the extra sts. into patt. Complete border I, 76 sts. Cont. in main patt., inc. likewise to 104—104—106—106 sts. When entire sleeve measures 15½—16—16½—17 ins., fin on a patt. rd., complete border II. Beg. as indicated. Inc. likewise 3 times, 110—110—112—112 sts. Finally inc. on the last 10 rds., 130—130—132—132 sts. Then turn the work inside out and k.6 rds. for seam facing. Cast off.

TO MAKE UP:

Press. Measure width of sleeve tops and mark corresponding length on Jumper for armholes. Make sure that patts. match at armholes. Machine twice around armholes in chain of sts., to prevent fraying, and cut between the machining. Fold facing at top on to wrong side and slip st. Join shoulders sewing through p.stripe. Leave 9 ins. open for neck. Attach sleeves carefully matching centres to shoulder seams. Sew through the p. stripe and in chain of sts. just beyond the machining around armholes. Press seam, fold facing over raw edges on wrong side and slip st. to neaten.

COLLAR:

Using set of needles no. 13 and W. cast on 120—120—124—124 sts. and work 6½ ins. in rib as before. Cast off loosely ribwise. Attach cast off edge to lower edge of facing. Fold collar outwards.

CAP:

Using set of needles no. 13 and M. or Dg. cast on 110 sts., all sizes and work in rib as for Jumper. Change to set of needles no. 10 and st.st. Inc. on first rd. to 121 sts. Complete border I. Cont. in main patt. until entire Cap measures 9½ ins. Next rd: K.2 sts. tog. throughout. Thread double wool through rem. sts.

TO MAKE UP:

Press. Draw tog. at top and fasten well. Make a large pompon and attach to crown.

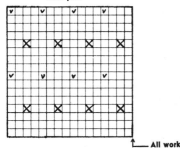

Main patt.

↑— All work

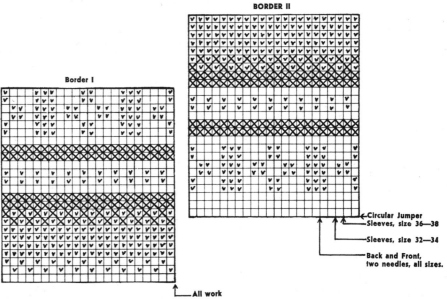

Border I

↑— All work

BORDER II

←Circular Jumper
Sleeves, size 36—38

—Sleeves, size 32—34

—Back and Front,
two needles, all sizes.

□ = White

V = Mustard or Dark green

X = Dark Brown or Light green

SHOWN IN COLOR ON PAGE 21.

LADY'S JUMPER

Size to fit 32—34—36—38 inch bust.

Materials:

	Size 32/34	36/38		
	10	11	balls	Black no. 502.
	3	3	«	White no. 501 or 17.
	3	3	«	Brown no. 821.

A pair of needles each no. 10 and 13 or 2 circular needles and set of needles each no. 10 and 13.

American		SIZE OF NEEDLES	0	3
British			13	10

44

TENSION:

26 stitches and 34 rows (30 in pattern) on no. 10 needles = 4 inches.
Check your tension very carefully. Adjust by using thicker or thinner needles.

ABBREVIATIONS:

Beg., beginning; cont., continue; dec., decrease; fin., finishing; inc., increase; inc. 1 st., pick up loop between sts. and k. into back of same; k., knit; patt., pattern; p., purl; rem., remaining; rd., round; sts., stitches; st.st., stocking stitch; B., Black.

TWO NEEDLE METHOD

BACK AND FRONT ALIKE:

Using no. 13 needles and B. cast on 120—126—136—136 sts. and work 1½ ins. in k. 1, p. 1 rib, fin. on wrong side. Change to no 10 needles and st.st. (k. on right, p. on wrong side). Size 32 and 34: Inc. 1 st. at beg. of first row. When entire work measures 14—15—16—17 ins., fin. on wrong side, cast off 10 sts. at beg. of next two rows for armholes. Place rem. 101—107—116—116 sts. on a holder.

SLEEVES:

Two sets of figures only, denote the first and last two sizes. Using no. 13 needles and B. cast on 62—66 sts. and work 2 ins. in rib as before, fin. on wrong side. Change to no. 10 needles and st.st. Inc. 1 st. within the first and last st. every 8th row until there are 100—106 sts. When entire sleeve measures 17—17½—18—19 ins., fin. on wrong side, cast off 10 sts. at beg. of next 2 rows. Leave the rem. 80—86 sts. on a holder.

YOKE — BACK:

Using no. 10 needles pick up 40—43 sts. (beg. at centre) from one Sleeve, entire Back, 40—43 sts. from the other Sleeve. 181—187—202—202 sts. in all. Work 6 rows.
N.B. for Size 34—36—38 dec. at regular intervals on third row until 181—201—201 sts. rem. Cont. in patt. from chart and dec. as indicated. K. together the following sts. throughout.
1st shaping: Size 32 and 34: 8th and 9th. 161 sts. rem.
   Size 36 and 38: 4th and 5th. 161 sts. rem.
2nd shaping: All sizes: 7th and 8th. 141 sts. rem.
3rd shaping: All sizes: 2nd and 3rd then 3rd and 4th alternately. 101 sts. rem.
4th shaping: All sizes: 4th and 5th. 81 sts. rem.
5th shaping: All sizes: 3rd and 4th. 61 sts. rem.
Complete the chart. Then work 5½ ins. in rib as before, for collar. Cast off ribwise.

YOKE — FRONT:

Work to match Back.

TO MAKE UP:

Darn in all loose ends. Omitting ribbing press work on wrong side with a hot iron over a damp cloth. Join together, edge to edge flat seams. Press all seams.

CIRCULAR KNITTING METHOD

BODY OF JUMPER:

Using circular needle no. 13 and B. cast on 240—252—270—270 sts. and work 1½ ins. in k. 1, p. 1 rib. Change to circular needle no. 10 and st.st. (k. all rds.). When entire work measures 14—15—16—17 ins. shape armholes: x. Cast off 10, k. 100—106—115—115, cast off 10 sts. Place a marker here. x. Repeat from x—x. Leave work aside.

SLEEVES:

Two sets of figures only, denote the first and last two sizes. Using set of no. 13 needles and B. cast on 62—66 sts. and work 2 ins. in rib as before. Change to set of no. 10 needles and st.st. Inc. 2 sts. at underarm, 1 st. either side of the first and last st. every 8th rd. until there are 100—106 sts. When entire sleeve measures 17—17½—18—19 ins. shape armholes: Cast off 10, k. 80—86, cast off 10 sts. Place on a holder.

YOKE:

Using circular needle no. 10 pick up 40—43 sts. (beg. at centre) from one Sleeve, entire Back, Sleeve, Front and rem. 40 sts. from Sleeve. 360—372—402—402 sts. K. 6 rds.
N.B. For size 34—36—38 dec. at regular intervals on third rd. until 360—400—400 sts. rem. Cont. in patt. from chart. Dec. as for Two Needle Method. Twice as many sts. minus two rem. Complete the chart then work 5½ ins. in rib as before. Cast off ribwise.

TO MAKE UP:

Darn in all loose ends. Press. Allow to dry. Join at underarms.

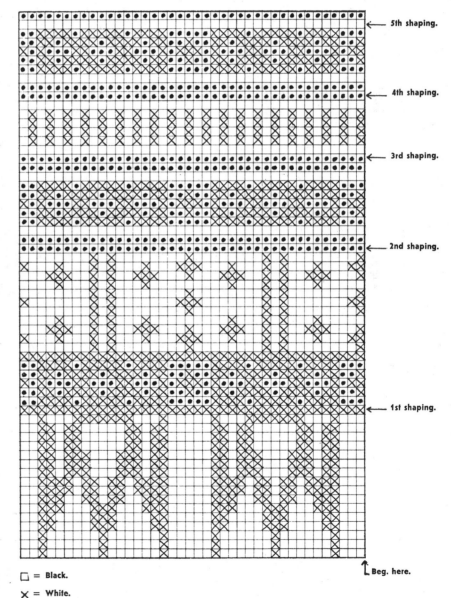

→ 5th shaping.
→ 4th shaping.
→ 3rd shaping.
→ 2nd shaping.
→ 1st shaping.
↳ Beg. here.

☐ = Black.

✕ = White.

● = Brown.

SHOWN IN COLOR ON INSIDE BACK COVER.

LADY'S JUMPER AND MAN'S JACKET

Size to fit 32-34-36-38 inch bust, 38-40-42-44 inch chest.

Materials:

Size 32/34	36/38			38	40/42	44	
8	9	balls White no. 501 or 17.	10	11	12 balls Charcoal no. 12.
4	4	« Mustard no. 748.	6	7	8 « Brown no. 739.
4	4	« Brown no. 741.	5	5	6 « White no. 17.

A pair of needles each no. 10 and 13 or 2 circular needles and set of needles each no. 10 and 13.

Actual measurements:

Size	32	34	36	38	38	40	42	44		
All round	36	36	40	40	41	44	44	46	ins.	approx.
Length	24	25	26	27	27	28	28	29	«	«
Sleeve seam	19	19	20	20	20	21	21	22	«	«

American		SIZE OF NEEDLES	0	3
British			13	10

TENSION:

26 stitches and 30 rows in pattern on no. 10 needles = 4 inches.

Check your tension very carefully. Adjust by using thicker or thinner needles.

ABBREVIATIONS:

Beg., beginning; cont., continue; dec., decrease; fin., finishing; inc., increase; inc. 1 st., pick up loop between sts. and k. into back of same; k., knit; patt., pattern; p., purl; rem., remaining; rep., repeat; rd., round; sts., stitches; st. st., stocking stitch; B., Brown.

TWO NEEDLE METHOD

LADY'S JUMPER:

Two sets of figures only, denote the first and last two sizes.

BACK AND FRONT ALIKE:

Using no. 13 needles and B. cast on 120—132 sts. and work 1½ ins. in k. 1, p. 1 rib, fin. on right side. P. 1 row, inc. 1 st. at beg. of same. Change to no. 10 needles and st. st. (k. on right, p. on wrong side). Cont. in patt. from chart, beg. as indicated. x. Complete border I. Cont. in main patt., beg. at 4th row and work 16 rows. Rep. border II three times with 5—6 ins., 7—8—8—8½ ins. approx. in main patt. fin. with a complete design between same. Having completed the third border II work 16 rows in main patt., rep. border I. Finally using B., k. 2 rows to form a p. stripe on right side, work 5 rows st. st. for facing. Cast off.

SLEEVES:

Using no. 13 needles and B. cast on 60 sts., all sizes, and work as for Jumper as far as x. Then inc. 1 st. within the first and last st. every 8th row, working the extra sts. into patt., until there are 101—103 sts. Cont. in same border sequence as for Jumper but with 5—6, 6—7 ins. approx. in main patt. between borders II. Inc. likewise on each of the last 10 rows of third border II. Rep. border I, inc. likewise on each row. 129—131 sts. Finally using B., k. 3 rows to form a p. stripe on right side. Cast off.

TO MAKE UP:

Darn in all loose ends. Omitting ribbing press work on wrong side with a hot iron over a damp cloth. Allow to dry. Join shoulders sewing through the p. stripe, leave 9 ins. open for neck. Slip st. around facing. Join sides and sleeves, edge to edge flat seams. Attach sleeves carefully matching centres to shoulders. Sew through the p. stripe and in second chain of sts. on Jumper. Press all seams.

MAN'S JACKET:

BACK:

Using no. 13 needles and B. cast on 132—144—144—156 sts. and work as for Jumper as far as x. Cont. in same border sequence also but with 6—7—8—8, 9—

9—9—9½ ins. in main patt. between borders II. Having completed the third border II work 16 rows in main patt. then rep. border I. Cont. in B., k. 1 row then work each shoulder separately. P. the next 44—49—49—51 sts., turn, p. 1 row on right side to form a stripe. Cast off. Cast off the rem. 45—47—47—55 sts. for neck.

RIGHT SIDE:

Using no. 13 needles and B. cast on 78—84—84—84 sts. and work the welt as before. P. to last 12 sts., inc. 1 st. for seam (to be worked in plain colour throughout) and place the rem. sts. on a holder for Front Band. Change to no. 10 needles and st. st. K. 1 row, inc. 1 st. Work in patt. to match Back. Having completed the third border II shape neck: Keeping continuity of patt. cast off the seam st. then 5—6—6—5 sts. Further dec. at beg. of k. rows 4—4—4—3 sts. then for all sizes 3 sts. twice, 2 sts. thrice, and 1 st. twice. 44—49—49—51 sts. rem. Cont. in B., p. 2 rows to form a stripe. Cast off.

LEFT SIDE:

Work the welt as for Right Front for 1 inch, fin. on right side. Next row: Rib 4, cast off 5 sts. for buttonhole, rib to end. On next row cast on 5 sts. over those cast off. Complete the welt, fin. on wrong side. Change to no. 10 needles. K. to last 12 sts., inc. 1 st. for seam, place the rem. sts. on a holder for Front Band. P. 1 row, inc. 1 st. Cont. to match Right Front. Beg. patt on k. row, neck shaping on p. rows.

SLEEVES:

Using no. 13 needles and B. cast on 72 sts., all sizes, and work as for Jumper sleeves but inc. to 113—115—117—117 sts. Also with 4, 4½—5—5—6 ins. in main patt. between borders II. Having completed the third border II work 16 rows in main patt. Inc. likewise on alternate rows twice then on each of the rem. 12 rows. 141—143—145—145 sts. Cont. in B., k. 3 rows to form a stripe. Cast off.

BUTTON BAND:

Using no. 13 needles and B. pick up the sts. from Right side, inc. 1 st. at inner edge for seam. Cont. in rib until band when slightly stretched reaches neckline. Cast off the seam st. and leave rem. sts. on a holder. Attach to Front. Mark position of buttons, spacing evenly, allow for 1 in neckband. (6 in all.)

BUTTONHOLE BAND:

Work to match making corresponding buttonholes as before. Attach to Front.

TO MAKE UP:

Proceed as for Jumper.

NECKBAND:

Using no. 13 needles and B. pick up 139—141—143—145 sts. around neckline, right side facing and work 2½ ins. in rib as before. Make a buttonhole after ½ inch and again after 1¾ ins. Cast off ribwise. Fold on to wrong side and slip st. Sew around buttonholes. Attach buttons. Press well.

CIRCULAR KNITTING METHOD

LADY'S JUMPER:

BODY OF JUMPER:

Using circular needle no. 13 and B. cast on 240—264 sts. and work 1½ ins. in k. 1, p. 1 rib. Change to st. st. (k. all rds.). K. 1 rd. Change to circular needle no. 10. Cont. in patt. from chart, beg. as indicated. Work in border sequence as for Two Needle Method. Finally using B., k. 1 rd., p. 1 rd., k. 5 rds. for facing. Cast off.

SLEEVES:

Using set of needles no. 13 and B. cast on 60 sts., all sizes and work the welt as before. K. 1 rd., inc. 1 st. Change to set of needles no. 10. Inc. 2 sts. at underarm, 1 st. either side of the first and last st. until there are 101—103 sts. Work in border sequence as for Two Needle Method and same shaping. Finally using B., k. 1 rd., p. 1 rd., k. 5 rds. for seam facing. Cast off.

TO MAKE UP:

Darn in all loose ends. Press. Measure width of sleeve tops and mark corresponding length on Jumper for armholes. Machine twice around armholes, to prevent fraying and cut between the machining. Join shoulders sewing through the p. stripe on right side, leave 9 ins. open for neck. Slip st. around facing. Attach sleeves carefully matching centres to shoulders. Sew through the p. stripe and in chain of sts. just beyond the machining around armholes. Press seam, fold over raw edges on wrong side and slip st. to neaten. Press well.

MAN'S JACKET:

BODY OF JACKET:

Using circular needle no. 13 and B. cast on 291—303—315—327 sts. and work 1 inch in k. 1, p. 1 rib, to and fro, fin. on right side. Next row: Rib 4, cast off 5 sts. for buttonhole, rib to end. On next row cast on 5 sts. over those cast off. Cont. in rib until welt measures 1½ ins., fin. on right side. Next row: Rib 13 sts., place on a holder, rib to last 13 sts., place on a holder for Front Band. Change to circular needle no. 10 and st. st. (k. all rds.). Cast on 3 sts. and join work into a rd. Work these sts. in plain colour throughout. The work is cut here later. Cont. in same border sequence as Two Needle Method. Having completed the third border II cont. in main patt.

On second rd. shape neck: Cast off the last 5—6—6—7 sts. From here work to and fro, p. on wrong side. Cast off the centre 3 sts., then 5—6—6—7 sts., k. to end. Further dec. at beg. of each row, for all sizes, 4 sts., 3 sts., 2 sts. thrice, 1 st. twice. 225—235—247—257 sts. rem. after 16 rows. Cont. in B. and work each shoulder separately. Allow 46—48—51—53 sts. for each. K. 2 rows, work 5 rows st. st. for facing. Cast off. Cast off rem. sts. for neck.

SLEEVES:

Using set of needles no. 13 and B. cast on 72 sts., all sizes, and work the welt as before. K. 1 rd., inc. 1 st. at beg. of same. Change to set of needles no. 10.

Inc. 2 sts. at underarm, 1 st. either side of the first and last st. until there are 113—115—117—117 sts. Work in border sequence as for Two Needle Method and same shaping. Finally using B., k. 1 rd., turn work inside out and k. 6 rds. for seam facing. Cast off.

BUTTON BAND:

Using no. 13 needles and B. cast on 5 sts. for facing, then pick up the 13 sts. from Right Front, right side facing. Cont. in rib but work the facing in st. st., until band when slightly stretched reaches to neckline. Then cast off the 5 sts., leave rem. sts. on a holder. Mark position of buttons, spacing evenly, allow for 1 in neckband. (6 in all).

BUTTONHOLE BAND:

Work to match making corresponding buttonholes as before.

TO MAKE UP:

Proceed as for Jumper. Machine twice along centre front and cut between the machining. Attach Front Bands. Press seam, fold facing over raw edges on wrong side and slip st. to neaten.

NECKBAND:

As for Two Needle Method. Press well. Attach buttons.

Main pattern

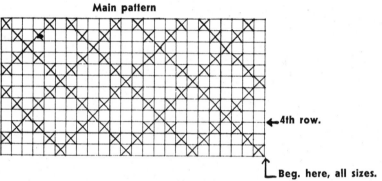

←4th row.

⌐Beg. here, all sizes.

Border II

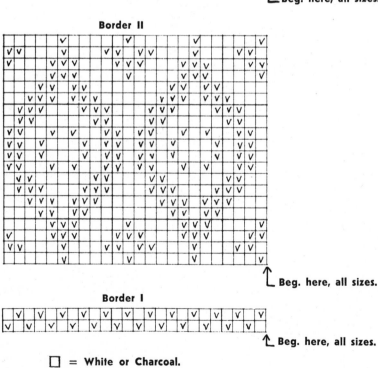

⌐Beg. here, all sizes.

Border I

⌐Beg. here, all sizes.

☐ = White or Charcoal.

V = Brown.

X = Mustard or White

LADY'S OR MAN'S SWEATER

Size to fit 32/34-36/38 inch bust, 38/40-40/42 inch chest.

Size	32/34	36/38		38/40	40/42	
	14	15	balls Red no. 813.	16	17	balls Brown no. 741.
or						
	14	15	« White no. 17.			
	2	2	« Black no. 502.			
	1	1	ball Brown no. 739.			

A pair of needles each no. 12 and 9.

American	SIZE OF NEEDLES	1	4
British		12	9

IOWN IN COLOR ON INSIDE FRONT COVER.

TENSION:
26 stitches and 34 rows in pattern on no. 9 needles = 4 inches.
Check your tension very carefully. Adjust by using thicker or thinner needles.

ABBREVIATIONS:
Beg., beginning; cont., continue; dec., decrease; fin., finishing; inc., increase; inc 1 st., pick up loop between sts. and k. into back of same; k., knit; patt., pattern; p., purl; rem., remaining; rep., repeat; sts., stitches; B., Black; Br., Brown; W., White.

PATTERN:
No. of sts. are divisible by 6 + 2.
1st row: (Right side) x K. 2, k. the second st. on left needle prior to first st, slip both sts. off needle. K. the next 2 sts. likewise but k. through back of second st. x Rep. from x—x throughout, end with k. 2.
2nd row: P.
Rep. these 2 rows throughout.

LADY'S RED SWEATER:
BACK:
Using no. 12 needles cast on 122—134 sts. and work 1½ ins. in k. 1, p. 1 rib, fin. on right side. P. 1 row. Change to no. 9 needles and patt. x. When entire work measures 16—16½ ins., fin. on wrong side, cast off 6 sts. at beg. of next 2 rows for armholes.

RAGLAN SHAPING:
Dec. 1 st. at beg. and end of right side every 4th row, 7 times then on every other row 25—29 times until 46—50 sts.

rem. for neck. Cont. thus: Right Side: Beg. on right side of work, work 5 sts., turn, cast off. Left side: Work 2 rows on rem. sts., cast off.

FRONT:
Work as Back to armholes.

RAGLAN SHAPING:
Dec. likewise every 4th row, 7 times then on every other row 18—22 times. Then place a marker at either side of the centre 10—14 sts. Cont. thus: Left side: (Dec. likewise on every other row 7 times more.) Work to first marker, turn, dec. at beg. of p. rows for neck, 4, 3, 2 sts. 4 times, 3 sts. for all sizes. Then cast off the 10—14 sts. between markers. Work Right side to match, reversing shapings.

SLEEVES:
Using no. 12 needles cast on 62 sts., all sizes and work 1½ ins in rib as before. P. 1 row. Change to no. 9 needles and patt. Inc. 1 st. within the first and last st. every 8th row, working the extra sts. into patt., until there are 96—104 sts. When entire sleeve measures 17½—18½ ins., fin. on wrong side cast off 6 sts. at beg. of next 2 rows. 84—92 sts. rem.

RAGLAN SHAPING:
Dec. as before on every other row until 6 sts. rem. for shoulder. Cast off Right sleeve on right side, Left on wrong side.

TO MAKE UP:
Press lightly on wrong side with a hot iron over a damp cloth. Allow to dry. Join together, edge to edge flat seams. Leave the left seam open on Back.

NECKBAND:
Using no. 12 needles pick up 124 sts. around neckline, right side facing and work 2 ins. in rib as before. Cast off loosely. Join Left seam and neckband. Fold neckband on to wrong side and slip st. Press seams.

LADY'S STRIPED SWEATER:
BACK:
Using no. 12 needles and B. cast on 122—134 sts. Work 1½ ins. in k. 1, p. 1 rib, 4 rows B., 2 rows Br. alternately. Fin. on right side. Cont. in W., p. 1 row. Change to no. 9 needles and patt. When entire work measures 10½—11½ ins. work the next 12 rows thus: 2 B., 4 W., 2 Br., 2 W., 2 B. Cont. in W. When entire work measures 16—16½ ins. complete as for previous Sweater.

FRONT:
Work as Back to armholes. Complete as for previous Sweater.

SLEEVES:
Using no. 12 needles and B. cast on 62 sts., all sizes and work the welt as before. Cont. in W., p. 1 row. Change to no. 9 needles and patt. Cont. as for previous sleeves. When entire sleeve measures 12—13 ins. work in stripes to match Sweater.

TO MAKE UP:
As previous Sweater. COLLAR: Work 6½ ins. in rib as before, 4 rows B., 2 rows Br. alternately, fin. with 4 rows B. Cast off loosely. Slip st. on wrong side.

MAN'S SWEATER:
BACK:
Using no. 12 needles cast on 140—146 sts. and work as Red Sweater as far as x. When entire work measures 16—17 ins., fin. on wrong side, cast off 6 sts. at beg. of next 2 rows. 128—134 sts. rem.

RAGLAN SHAPING:
Dec. 1 st. at beg. and end of right side of work every 4th row, 4 times then every other row until 48—50 sts. rem., fin. on wrong side. Right side: Work 5 sts., turn, cast off. Cast off the centre 38—40 sts. Work Left side to match. Cast off on right side.

FRONT:
Work as Back to armholes.

RAGLAN SHAPING:
Dec. as before, every 4th row, 4—4 times. 120—126 sts. rem. Place a marker at exact centre. Left side: Cont. raglan as on Back. On first row work to marker, turn. Dec. here for V neck. Dec. 1 st. at beg. of every p. row 24—25 times. (On the last 24—26 rows dec. only for raglans.) Work the Right side to match, reversing shapings.

SLEEVES:
Using no. 12 needles cast on 68 sts., all sizes. Work as Lady's sleeves until there are 106—110 sts. When entire sleeve measures 18½—19 ins., fin. on wrong side, cast off 6 sts. at beg. of next 2 rows.

RAGLAN SHAPING:
Dec. as for Lady's sleeves until 6 sts. rem. Cast off likewise.

TO MAKE UP:
As Lady's Sweater.

NECKBAND:
Using no. 12 needles pick up 142—148 sts. around neckline. Place a marker at base of V neck. Work 1 inch in rib as before. The centre st. at marker must be a k. st. Dec. 1 st. at either side of same on every row. Cast off. Join seam and Left raglan. Press all seams.

SHOWN IN COLOR ON INSIDE BACK COVER.

LADY'S JUMPER WITH V OR ROUND NECK, AND SKIRT

Size to fit 32—34—36—38 inch bust.

Materials:

Jumper: Size 32 34 36 38

10	11	12	13	balls White no. 501 or 17 or Brown no. 769.
1	1	2	2	« Brown no. 769 or White no. 501 or 17.
1	1	1	1	ball Charcoal no. 12.

Skirt: 8 9 9 10 balls Brown no. 769 or White no. 501 or 17.

A pair of needles each no. 10 and 13 and a spare needle with points both ends or 2 circular and set of needles each no. 10 and 13, short circular needle no. 13.

Actual measurements:

Jumper:					
	All round	36	36	38	38 ins.
	Length	23	24	25	26 «
	Sleeve seam	17	17½	18	19 «
Skirt:	Hips	35	37	39	41 ins.
	Length	25	25½	26	26½ «

American		SIZE OF NEEDLES	0	3
British			13	10

TENSION:
26 stitches and 34 rows plain (30 in pattern) on no. 10 needles = 4 inches.

Check your tension very carefully. Adjust by using thicker or thinner needles.

50

ABBREVIATIONS:
Beg., beginning; cont., continue: dec., decrease; fin., finishing; inc., increase; inc. 1 st., pick up loop between sts. and k. into back of same; k., knit; Mc., Main colour; patt., pattern; p., purl; rem., remaining; rep., repeat; rd., round; sts., stitches; st.st., stocking stitch; tog., together.

TWO NEEDLE METHOD
JUMPER WITH V NECK

BACK:
Two sets of figures only, denote the first and last two sizes. Using no. 13 needles and Mc. cast on 121—133 sts. and work in st.st. throughout, (k. on right, p. on wrong side). Work 12 rows, p 1 row on right side for hem, work 12 rows more. Cont. in border patt. from chart, beg. as indicated.
Size 32 and 34: Complete same. **Size 36 and 38:** Work the first 11 rows then dec. 1 st. within the first and last st. and work the next 15 rows. Inc. likewise and complete the patt. Cont. in Mc., dec. likewise on second row. 131 sts. rem.
When work measures 14½—15—15½—15½ ins. from p. stripe, fin. on wrong side, shape armholes. At beg. of next 2 rows cast off 7—8 sts. 107—115 sts. rem. x.
Size 38: Work 6 rows. xx.

RAGLAN SHAPING:
K.1, k.2 tog. through back of sts., k. to last 3, k.2 tog., k.1 st. Dec. likewise on every k. row until 39—43 sts. rem. for neck. Cast off.

FRONT:
As Back to xx. Then place a marking thread in the centre st. for base of V.

RAGLAN AND V NECK SHAPING:
Left side: Dec. for raglan, k. to st. before marking thread, turn p.1, p.2 tog., p. to end. Cont. to dec. as for Back at beg. of every k. row 33—35 times altogether and dec. 1 st., within the first st., at beg. of every 4th p. row for neck 17—18 times altogether until 3—4 sts. rem. Fin. on a p. row. Cast off knitwise.
Right side: K.2 tog., k.1, k.2 tog., k. to last 3, k.2 tog., k.1 st. Cont. to match Left side. Reverse shapings, dec. at the end of every k. row and at beg. of every 4th k. row. Fin. on a k. row. Cast off purlwise.

SLEEVES:
Using no. 13 needles and Mc. cast on 54—54—56—58 sts. and work 2 ins. in k.1, p.1 rib, fin. on wrong side. Change to no. 10 needles and st.st. Inc 1 st. within the first and last st. at both sides every 6th row until there are 96—100 sts. When entire sleeve measures 17—17½—18—18½ ins., fin on wrong side, shape armholes. At beg. of next 2 rows cast off 8 sts. for all sizes. 80—84 sts. rem.
Size 38: Work 6 rows.

RAGLAN SHAPING:
Dec. as on Back on every k. row until 12 sts. rem. Cast off knitwise on Right, purlwise on Left sleeve.

TO MAKE UP:
Darn in all loose ends. Omitting ribbing press work on wrong side with a hot iron over a damp cloth. Allow to dry. Join together, edge to edge flat seams. Leave Left raglan on Back open.

NECKBAND:
Using no. 13 needles pick up and k.150 —158 sts. around neckline, right side facing. Place a marker in the centre st. at base of V. Work 1 inch in k.1, p.1 rib. N.B. The centre st. must be a k. st. K.2 tog. either side of same on every row. Cast off ribwise. Join rem. seam, neckband and underarms. Fold hem on to wrong side and slip st. Press all seams.

JUMPER WITH ROUND NECK

BACK:
As V Jumper to x. 107—115 sts. Then work 4—4—4—10 rows without shaping.

RAGLAN SHAPING:
1st row: K.1, k.2 tog., k. to last 3, k.2 tog. through back of sts., k.1 st.
2nd and 4th row: P. without shaping.
3rd row: K.1, k.2 tog., k.1, place the next 2 sts. on spare needle and leave at back of work. K.2, k. the sts. from spare needle, k. to last 8, place the next 2 sts. on spare needle and leave at front of work. K.2, k. the sts. from spare needle, k.1, k.2 tog. through back of sts., k.1 st. Rep. these 4 rows until 43—47 sts. rem. Cast off.

FRONT:
As Back. When 47—51 sts. rem. Cast off.

SLEEVES:
As previous ones as far as x. Then work 4—4—10 rows without shaping.

RAGLAN SHAPING:
Dec. as on Back on every k. row until 18 sts. rem. Cast off knitwise on Right, purlwise on Left sleeve.

TO MAKE UP:
As for V Jumper.

NECKBAND:
Using no. 13 needles pick up and k.116 —120 sts. around neckline, right side facing. Work 2 ins. in k.1, p.1 rib. Cast off. Fold on to wrong side and slip st. Press all seams.

CIRCULAR KNITTING METHOD

JUMPER WITH V NECK

BODY OF JUMPER:
Using circular needle no. 13 and Mc. cast on 240—258 sts. and work in st.st. throughout, (k. all rds.). K.12 rds., p.1 rd. for hem, k.12 rds. more. Cont. in border patt. from chart, beg. as indicated.
Size 36 and 38: On 12th rd. inc. 1 st. after first and 129 th st. Dec. likewise on 25th rd. Complete the patt. Cont. in Mc., dec. likewise on second rd. When work measures 14½—15—15½—15½ ins. from p. stripe shape armholes. x Cast off 7—8, k.106—114, cast off 7—8, k.106—114, cast off 7—8 sts. Place a marker here to denote side. x Rep. from x—x. Leave work aside.

SLEEVES:
Using set of needles no. 13 and Mc. cast on 54—54—56—58 sts. and work 2 ins. in k.1, p.1 rib. Cont. in st.st. K.1 rd. Change to set of needles no. 10. Inc. 2 sts. at underarm, 1 st. at either side of the first and last st. every 6th rd. until there are 96—100 sts. When entire sleeve measures 17—17½—18—19 ins. shape armhole. Cast off 7—8, k.82—84, cast off 7—8 sts. leave on a holder.

YOKE:
Using circular needle no. 10 k. the work on to same as follows: Back, Sleeve, Front, Sleeve. Slip the sts. so that the centre st. of Front comes at beg. of rd. K.1 rd. and k.2 sts. tog. where each piece meets. Place a marker here to denote where to shape. 372—392 sts.
Size 38: K. 6 rds.
Work to and fro here. P. on wrong side. Dec. for neck and raglans as follows:
V NECK:
Dec. 1 st. within the first and last st. on every 4th row 17—18 times. Work to and fro here. P. on wrong side.

RAGLAN SHAPING:
x K. to last 2 sts. before marker, k.2 tog., k.2 tog. through back of sts. x. Rep. from x—x 3 times. Cont. thus on every k. row until 66—68 sts. rem.

NECKBAND:
Using short circular needle no. 13 pick up 41—43 sts. along Right side, the rem. 66—68 sts. and 41—43 sts. along Left side. Work 1 inch in k.1, p.1 rib. N.B. the centre st. at base of V must be a k. st. K.2 tog. either side of same on every rd. Cast off ribwise.

TO MAKE UP:
Press. Join underarms. Fold hem on to wrong side and slip st. Press well.

JUMPER WITH ROUND NECK

BODY OF JUMPER AND SLEEVES:
As for V Jumper.

YOKE:
As for V Jumper but beg. rds. at first marker on Back. 372—392 sts. Then k. 4—4—4—10 rds. without shaping.

RAGLAN SHAPING:
1st rd.: x K.2 tog., k. to last 2 sts. before next marker, k.2 tog. through back of sts. x Rep. from x—x 3 times. Dec. 8 sts. in all).
2nd and 4th rd: K. without shaping.
3rd rd.: x k.2 tog., k.1, place the next 2 sts. on spare needle and leave at back of work. K.2, k. the sts. from spare needle. K. to last 7 sts. before next marker, place the next 2 sts. on to spare needle and leave at front of work. K.2, k. the sts. from spare needle, k.1, k.2 tog. through back of sts. x Rep. from x—x 3 times.
Rep. these 4 rds. until 116—120 sts. rem.

NECKBAND:
Change to set of no. 13 needles and work 2 ins. in k.1, p.1 rib. Cast off loosely.

TO MAKE UP:
As previous Jumper. Fold neckband on to wrong side and slip st. Press well.

SKIRT
TWO NEEDLE METHOD

BACK AND FRONT ALIKE:
Using no. 10 needles and Mc. cast on 116—122—130—138 sts. and work in st. st. throughout. Work 12 rows, p.1 row on right side for hem. When work measures 15½—16—16½—17 ins. from p. stripe beg. shapings. K.2 tog. within the first and last 2 sts., every 8th row 6 times. Then on every 4th row 9—9—12 —13 times. 86—92—94—100 sts. rem. Cont. without further shaping until work measures 23½—24½—25—26 ins. (or length required) from p. stripe. Change to no. 13 needles and work 1 inch in k.1, p.1 rib. Cast off ribwise.

TO MAKE UP:
Press. Join sides, edge to edge flat seams. Leave 8 ins. open in Left side for zipp fastener. Slip st. around hem. Sew in zipp fastener. Attach elastic, according to waist measurement, to ribbing at top of skirt. Press all seams.

CIRCULAR KNITTING METHOD

Using circular needle no. 10 and Mc. cast on 230—244—260—276 sts. and work in st.st. throughout. K.12 rds., p.1 rd. for hem. When work measures 13—13½—14—14½ ins. from p. stripe beg. shapings. Place a marker at beg. of rd. and another after 115—122—130—138 sts. to denote sides. K.2 sts. tog. at both sides of same every 8th rd. 14 times. 174—188—204—220 sts. rem. Cont. without further shaping until work measures 23½—24½—25—26 ins. (or length required) form p. stripe. Change to circular needle no. 13 and work 1 inch in k.1, p.1 rib. Cast off ribwise.

TO MAKE UP:
Press Slip st. around hem. Attach elastic as for Two needle method.

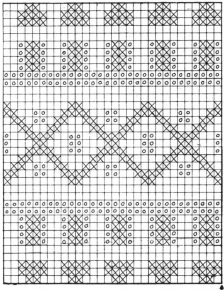

□ = White or Brown.
✕ = Brown or White.
o = Charcoal.

Begin all work here.

SHOWN IN COLOR ON PAGE 26.

LADY'S AND MAN'S STOCKINGS, MITTENS, AND GLOVES

Materials:

Stockings:
3—4 Balls Blue no. 584 or Grey no. 7.
2—2 « White no. 501 or 17.

Mittens:
2—2 Balls Blue no. 584 or Grey no. 7.
1—1 « White no. 501 or 17.

Gloves:
2—2 Balls Blue no. 584 or Grey no. 7.
1—1 « White no. 501 or 17.
A set of needles each no. 10, 11 and 13.
(American, 3, 2, and 0.)

TENSION:

26 stitches and 30 rows in pattern on
no. 10 needles = 4 inches.
**Check your tension very carefully.
Adjust by using thicker or thinner
needles.**

ABBREVIATIONS:

Beg., beginning; cont., continue; dec.,
decrease; fin., finishing; inc., increase;
inc. 1 st., pick up loop between sts. and
k. into back of same; k., knit; patt.,
pattern; p., purl; rem., remaining; rep.,
repeat; rd., round; sts., stitches; st. st.,
stocking stitch; tog., together; Mc., Main
colour; W., White.

STOCKINGS:

Using set of no. 13 needles and Mc.
cast on 86—98 sts. Work in st. st. (k. all
rds.). K. 4 rds. On next rd. cast off 2
sts. at beg. and end of rd. On next rd.
cast on 4 sts. over those cast off. K. 2
rds. then work as follows: (K. 2 tog.,

pass wool over needle) rep. throughout.
x. K. 9 rds. inc. 1 st. at end of last rd.
Change to set of needles no. 10. Cont.
in main patt., beg. and end the rds.
with 1 st. W., apart from patt. When
work measures 4½—5½ ins. from x beg.
shaping. Dec. 1 st. (k. 2 tog.) within
the first and last st. every 8th rd., 16—
16 times, until 55—67 sts. rem. Cont.
without further shaping until work
measures 14—16 ins. from x.

HEEL:

Work to and fro, p. on wrong side.
Cont. in patt. II thus: K. 14 sts., turn,
p. back, p. 14 sts. at opposite side of
rd. Work 2 ins. on these 28 sts., fin. on
wrong side.

HEEL SHAPING:

K. 19 sts., turn, (slip the first st. always) k. 10 sts., turn. Work to last st. before the hole, k. 2 tog., k. 1 st., turn. Cont. likewise until 18 sts. rem. From here work in rds. again. K. 9 sts., place a marker here, to denote centre of heel. Further rds. beg. here. Pick up 12 sts. at either side of heel. K. 19 sts., through back of loops, in patt. II, k. 2 tog. likewise. K. the 27—39 instep sts. in main patt. as before. Work the first and last st. here in Mc. Slip the next st., k. 1 st., through back of loop, pass the slip st. over. K. the next. 19 sts., through back of loops, in patt. II. Cont. working the instep in main patt., rem. sts. in patt. II as usual. At the same time dec. 1 st. at beg. and end of patt. II on alternate rds. until 61—65 sts. rem. When foot measures 8½—9½ ins. cont. entirely in patt. II. Dec. 1 st. both sides of each side st. until 9 sts. rem. Draw wool through sts. and fasten well.

TO MAKE UP:

Darn in all loose ends. Press with a hot iron over a damp cloth. Allow to dry. Fold over in row of holes and slip st. Thread elastic in top.

MITTENS:

Using set of needles no. 13 and Mc. cast on 52—60 sts. and work in k. 1, p. 1 rib. After 1 inch work the next 11 rds. thus: 3 W., 2 Mc., 1 W., 2 Mc., 3 W. Then work 1 inch in Mc. Change to no. 11 needles and st. st. K. 2 rds., first rd. of patt. II, 1 rd. Mc.

RIGHT MITTEN:

K. 3 sts. in patt. IV, 3 in Mc., 1 in W., 15—19 in patt. III, 3 in patt. IV, 27—31 sts. in patt. I. (2 sts. in Mc. here for size 1, 4 sts. in Mc. for size 2). K. 4 rds. On next rd. k. 6, inc. 1, k. 1 st., inc. 1, k. to end. Inc. likewise every 6th rd. for size 1, every 5th rd. for size 2 (for thumb) as shown on chart, until there are 6—8 extra sts. Then k. 2—1 rds. Next rd., all sizes: K. 5, place the next 9—11 on a holder, cast on 9—11 sts., k. to end. 58—68 sts. Cont. thus: K. 3 in patt. IV, 25—31 in patt. III, 3 in patt. IV, 27—31 sts. in patt. I.
Work 4½—5 ins. Then for size 1 dec. 1 st. either side of patt. I. 25 sts. rem. For both sizes dec. 1 st. either side of the 3 sts. in patt. IV, (4 in all) until 8—12 sts. rem. Draw wool through sts. and fasten well.

THUMB:

Pick up the 9—11 sts. from holder also same no. from cast on edge opposite, and 1 st. at each side. 20—24 sts. K. 1 W., 9—11 in patt. III, placing first or third st. of design in centre, 1 W., 9—11 sts. in patt. III. Work 2½ ins. Then dec. 1 st. either side of the W. st. every rd. (4 in all) until 4 sts. rem. Draw wool through sts. and fasten well.

LEFT MITTEN:

Work to match Right Mitten. Beg. patts. thus: K. 27—31 sts. in patt. I, 3 in patt. IV, 15—19 in patt. III, 1 W., 3 Mc., 3 sts. in patt. IV. Inc. 1 st. either side of the 1 st W. for Thumb.

GLOVES:

Work as for Mittens as far as 13th—15th rd. after Thumb opening.

RIGHT GLOVE:

1st Finger: Cont. on the first 10—11 and last 6—8 sts. of rd., cast on 4—3 sts. between same. 20—22 sts. Place rem. sts. on a holder. K. 3 sts. at both sides in patt. IV, k. the 7—8 sts. between same either side in patt. III. Work 3—3¼ ins. Then dec. 1 st. either side of the 3 sts. (4 in all) until 8—6 sts. rem. Draw wool through sts. and fasten well.
2nd Finger: Cont. on the next 7—8 sts. either side, cast on 3 sts. at both sides. 20—22 sts. Work 3¼—3½ ins, complete as before.
3rd Finger: Cont. on the next 7—8 sts. either side, cast on 3 sts. at both sides. 20—22 sts. K. 3 sts., either side in patt. IV, rem. sts. in patt. III. Work 3—3¼ ins. Complete as before.
4th Finger: Cont. on the last 14—17 sts., cast on 3 sts. between same. Work 2½ ins. and complete as 3rd Finger.
THUMB: As for Mitten.

LEFT GLOVE:

Work to match Right Glove. Divide sts. as for Left Mitten.

TO MAKE UP:

Darn in all loose ends. Press well.

Patt. IV

Patt. III

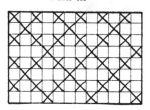

Patt. II

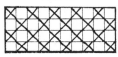

Patt. I

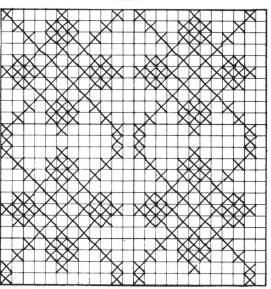

MAN'S Thumb

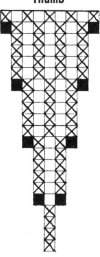

LADY'S Thumb

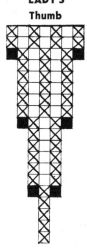

☐ = Blue or Grey.
✕ = White.
■ = Inc. 1 st.

SHOWN IN COLOR ON PAGE 23.

LADY'S JUMPER AND SKIRT

Size to fit 34—36 inch bust, 36 inch hips.

Materials:

Size	34	36		
	16	17	balls	White no. 17
	7	7	«	Mustard no. 748
	2	2	«	Charcoal no. 12
	2	2	«	Red no 681

A pair of needles no. 10 or a circular needle and set of needles each no. 10.

American		SIZE OF NEEDLES	3
British			10

Measurements:	Bust	35½—38	ins.
	Length	22½—23½	«
	Sleeve	13½—14	«
	SKIRT:		
	Waist	25½—26½	«
	Hips	38 —38	«
	Length	24½—25½	«

TENSION:
26 stitches and 32 rows in main pattern on no. 10 needles = 4 inches.

Check your tension very carefully. Adjust by using thicker or thinner needles.

ABBREVIATIONS:
Beg., beginning; cont., continue; dec., decrease; fin., finishing; inc., increase; inc. 1 st., pick up loop between sts. and k. into back of same; k., knit; patt., pattern; p., purl; rem., remaining; rep.,

repeat; rd., round; sts., stitches; st.st., stocking stitch; C., Charcoal; Mc., Main colour.

TWO NEEDLE METHOD
JUMPER:

BACK AND FRONT ALIKE:
Using C. cast on 118—127 sts. Work in st.st. throughout (k. on right, p. on wrong side). Work 8 rows, p.1 row on right side for hem. Cont. in patt. from chart, beg. as indicated. Complete border I, cont. in main patt. until work measures 14½—15½ ins. from p. stripe. Then shape armholes: Cast off 4 sts. at beg. of next 2 rows then 1 st. at both sides on alternate rows 10 times until 90—99 sts. rem. Cont. on these sts. until work measures 22½—23½ ins. from p. stripe. Then place 18—22 sts. at both sides for shoulders and rem. 54—55 sts. on separate holders.

SLEEVES:
Using C. cast on 73 sts. Work the hem as for Jumper. Cont. in patt. Complete border II. Cont. in main patt. but inc. 1 st. at both sides every 10th row, working the extra sts. into patt., until there are 97—99 sts. When sleeve measures 13½—14 ins. from p. stripe shape armhole. Cast off 4 sts. at beg. of next 2 rows then 1 st. at both sides on alternate rows 5 times until 69—71 sts. rem. Finally p.1 row on right side (k. on wrong side), work 1 more row and cast off.

TO MAKE UP:
Darn in all loose ends. Omitting ribbing press work on wrong side with a hot iron over a damp cloth. Allow to dry. Join sides and sleeves, edge to edge flat seams. Graft right shoulder. Collar: Pick up the sts. from holders, right side facing. Dec. the larger size to 108 sts. Complete border II. Cont. in C. only, p.1 row on right side, work 8 rows st.st. for facing. Cast off. Join left shoulder and collar. Attach sleeves carefully matching centres to shoulders. Sew through the p. stripe and through the second chain of sts. on Jumper. Slip st. around hems and collar. Press all seams.

SKIRT

BACK AND FRONT ALIKE:
Using C. cast on 127 sts. Work the hem as for Jumper. Cont. in patt., beg. as indicated. Complete border II, cont. in main patt. until work measures 16½—17½ ins. from p. stripe.

SHAPING:
Dec. 1 st. at both sides (within the first and last st.) on alternate rows 10 times. Rep. likewise on every 4th row 11—9 times until 85—89 sts. rem. Cont. on these sts. until work measures 24½—25½ ins. from p. stripe (or length required). Cont. in Mc. only and work 1 inch in k.1, p.1 rib. Cast off loosely.

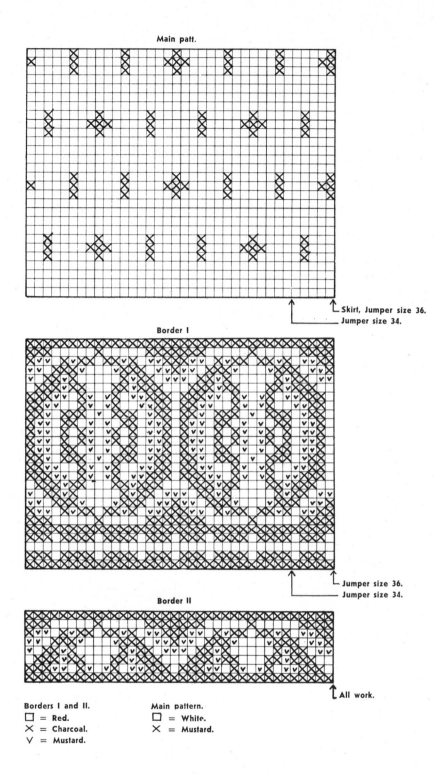

Main patt.

Skirt, Jumper size 36.
Jumper size 34.

Border I

Jumper size 36.
Jumper size 34.

Border II

All work.

Borders I and II.
☐ = Red.
✕ = Charcoal.
∨ = Mustard.

Main pattern.
☐ = White.
✕ = Mustard.

rds. 10 times until 89—98 sts. rem. between the markers, for Back and Front. Cont. on these sts. until work measures 22½—23½ ins. from stripes. Next rd.: Cast off the first extra 3 sts. x K. the following sts. and place on separate holders, 18—22, the centre 53—54, 18—22. x. Cast off the next 3 sts. Rep. from x—x. Leave work aside.

SLEEVES:

Using set of needles no. 10 and C. cast on 73 sts. Work the hem as for Jumper. Cont. in patt. Complete border II. Cont. in main patt. but inc. 2 sts. at underarm, 1 st. at either side of the first and last st. of rd. every 10th rd., working the extra sts. into patt. until there are 97—99 sts. When sleeve measures 13½—14 ins. from p. stripe shape armhole: Cast off 4, k.89—91, cast off 4 sts. From here work to and fro (k. on right, p. on wrong side). Dec. 1 st. at both sides 5 times, then dec. likewise on alternate rows 5 times until 69—71 sts. rem. Finally in Mc. only p.1 row on right side (k. on wrong side), work 5 rows st.st. for facing. Cast off.

TO MAKE UP:

Darn in all loose ends. Press. Machine twice around armholes to prevent fraying, in the extra sts. allowed for same and cut between the machining. Graft shoulders.
Collar: Using circular needle pick up sts. from holders, right side facing. Inc. the smaller size to 108 sts. Complete border II. Cont. in C. only, p.1 rd., k.8 rds. for facing. Cast off. Slip st. around hems and collar. Attach sleeves carefully matching centres to shoulders. Sew through the p. stripe and in chain of sts. just beyond the machining around armholes. Press seam, fold facing over raw edges on wrong side and slip st. to neaten.

SKIRT

Using circular needle no. 10 and C. cast on 252 sts. Work the hem as for Jumper. Cont. in patt., beg. as indicated. Complete border II, cont. in main patt. until work measures 16½—17½ ins. from p. stripe.

SHAPING:

Place a marking thread at beg. of rd. and one after 126 sts. Dec. 1 st. after each marker so that 125 sts. rem. for Back and Front. Dec. 1 st. either side of each marker (4 in all) every 5th rd. 14—12 times until 97—101 sts. rem. at both sides. Cont. until work measures 24½—25½ ins. from p. stripe (or length required). Cont. in Mc. only, k.8 rds., p.1 rd., k.8 rds. for hem. Cast off.

TO MAKE UP:

Darn in all loose ends. Press. Slip st. around hems. Thread elastic according to waist measurement in top of skirt. Press well.

TO MAKE UP:

Darn in all loose ends. Press. Join sides, edge to edge flat seams, leaving 8½ ins. open for zipp fastener. Slip st. around hem. Sew in zipp fastener. Attach elastic according to waist measurement to ribbing at top of skirt. Press all seams.

CIRCULAR KNITTING METHOD

BODY OF JUMPER:

Using circular needle no. 10 and C. cast on 234—252 sts. Work in st.st. throughout (k. all rds.). K.8 rds., p.1 rd. for hem. Cont. in patt. from chart, beg. as indicated. Complete border I, cont. in main patt. until work measures 14½—15½ ins. from p. stripe. Then shape armholes: Cast off 4, k.109—118, cast off 4 sts. Place a marking thread here to denote right side. Rep. on rem. half. Place another marker to denote left side. Cont. in main patt. Cast on 3 sts. at both sides over each marker and work these sts. in Mc. throughout. The work is cut here later for armholes. Then shape armholes: Dec. 1 st. at both sides of the extra 3 sts. (4 in all) on alternate

SHOWN IN COLOR ON BACK COVER.

LADY'S AND MAN'S SWEATERS

Size to fit 34-34/36-38 inch bust, 38-40/42-44 inch chest.

Materials:

LADIES:
Size 34 34/36 38

11	12	13	balls White no. 501 or 17.
1	1	1	ball Blue no. 584.
1	1	1	ball Red no. 140

MEN:
38 40/42 44

14	14/15	16	balls Blue no. 584.
2	2/2	2	» Red no. 140.
1	1/2	2	« White no. 501.

A pair of needles each no. 10 and 13 or 2 circular needles and set of needles each no. 10 and 13.

American		SIZE OF NEEDLES	0 3
British			13 10

Actual measurements:

Size	34	34 /36	38	38	40 /42	44	
All round	35½	35½/40	40	41	44 /44	46½	ins.
	34	36 /38	40	42½	44½/44½	46½	Circular.
Length	24½	25 /26	26½	27	27½/28	29	
Sleeve seam	17	17½/18	18½	19	19½/20	20	

TENSION:

26 stitches and 34 rows plain (30 rows pattern) on no. 10 needles = 4 inches. **Check your tension very carefully. Adjust by using thicker or thinner needles.**

ABBREVIATIONS:

Beg., beginning; cont., continue; dec., decrease; fin., finishing; inc., increase; inc. l st., pick up loop between sts. and k. into back of same; k., knit; patt., pattern; p., purl; rem., remaining; rep., repeat; rd., round; sts., stitches; st.st., stocking stitch; tog., together; Mc., Main colour.

TWO NEEDLE METHOD
LADY'S SWEATER

BACK AND FRONT ALIKE:

Using no. 13 needles and Mc. cast on 118—118 / 132—132 sts. and work 2 ins. in k.1, p.1 rib, fin. on wrong side. Change to no. 10 needles and st.st. (k. on right, p. on wrong side). Inc. 1 st. on first row. x When entire work measures 6½—7/7½—7½ ins., fin. on wrong side complete the border patt., from chart. Beg. as indicated, work the first and last st. alike. Cont. in Mc. When entire work measures 15½—16/17—17½ ins., fin. on wrong side, shape armholes. Cast off 8—8/9—9 sts. at beg. of next 2 rows. 103—103/115—115 sts.

RAGLAN SHAPING:

K.1, slip 1, k.1, pass the slip st. over, k. to the last 3 sts., k.2 tog., k.1. Dec. likewise on every 4th row 7—8/5—6 times, then on every k. row 22—21/28 —27 times until 45—45/49—49 sts. rem. for neck. Place on a holder.

RIGHT SLEEVE:

Using no. 13 needles and Mc. cast on 58—60/64—66 sts. and work as for Back as far as x. Then inc. 1 st. at both sides every 8th row until there are 95—97/ 101—105 sts. When entire sleeve measures 17—17½/18—19 ins. fin. on wrong side, shape armhole. Cast off 8—8/9—9 sts. at beg. of next 2 rows. 79—81 / 83—87 sts.

RAGLAN SHAPING:

Dec. as for Back every 4th row 8—8/ 9—9 times then on every k. row 20—19/ 20—21 times. 23—25/25—27 sts. Leave sts. on a holder.

LEFT SLEEVE:

Work as for Right but dec. on p. rows.

TO MAKE UP:

Darn in all loose ends. Omitting ribbing press work on wrong side with a hot iron over a damp cloth. Allow to dry. Join together, edge to edge flat seams but leave the Left Raglan on Back open for the time being.

COLLAR:

Using no. 10 needles and Mc. pick up the sts. around neckline, right side facing and adjust on first row to 136—140/

144—144 sts. Work ½ inch. in k.1, p.1 rib, fin. on right side. Then k.1 row on wrong side, k.1 row, p.1 row. Work the first 14 rows of border patt. K.1 row, p.1 row, p.1 row on right side, work 7 rows st.st. for facing. Cast off. Press lightly. Join Left seam and collar. Press all seams.

MAN'S SWEATER

BACK:

Using no. 13 needles and Mc. cast on 136—146/146—154 sts. and work 2 ins. in k.1, p.1 rib, fin. on wrong side. Change to no. 10 needles and st.st. (k. on right, p. on wrong side). Inc. 1 st. on first row. When entire work measures

12—13/13—14 ins., fin. on wrong side, complete the border patt. from chart, beg. as indicated. Work the first 39 rows then shape armholes. Cast off 10—10/ 10—11 sts. at beg. of next 2 rows. 117 —127/127—133 sts.

RAGLAN SHAPING:

K.1, slip 1, k.1, pass the slip st. over, k. to the last 3 sts., k. 2 tog., k.1. Dec. likewise every 4th row 6—3/6—5 times (complete the patt. and cont. in Mc.) then on every k. row 28—35/32—35 times until 49—51/51—53 sts. rem. for neck. Place on a holder.

Border pattern.

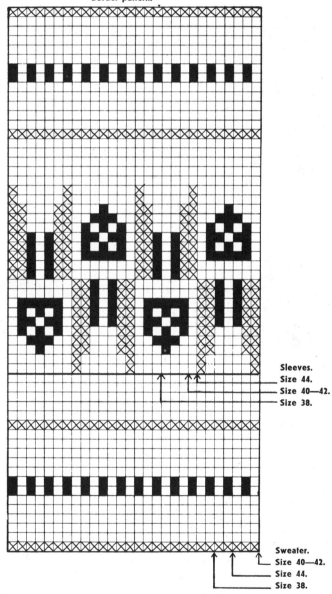

Sleeves.
Size 44.
Size 40—42.
Size 38.

Sweater.
Size 40—42.
Size 44.
Size 38.

Begin Ladies Sweaters and Circular Knitting as size 40—42.

	Ladies	Men
☐ =	White	Blue.
✕ =	Blue.	Red.
■ =	Red.	White

FRONT:

Work as Back as far as RAGLAN SHAPING, cont. as follows: Dec. on every 4th row 4—1/4—3 times then on every k. row 30—37/34—37 times until 49—51/51—53 sts. rem. Place on a holder.

RIGHT SLEEVE:

Using no. 13 needles and Mc. cast on 60—60/64—66 sts. Work as for Back as far as x. Then inc. 1 st. at both sides every 8th row until there are 91—91/97—99 sts. When entire sleeve measures 13—14/14½—15 ins. cont. in border patt. Work the first 19 rows, inc. likewise every 6th row until there are 97—97/103—105 sts. Cont. in patt., beg. as indicated. Inc. likewise, complete the next 20 rows then shape armhole. Cast off 10—10/11—11 sts. at beg. of next 2 rows. 85—85/89—91 sts. Complete the patt. at the same time shaping as follows:

RAGLAN SHAPING:

Dec. as for Back every 4th row 4—5/7—7 times then on every k. row 31—35/29—30 times until 15—15/17—17 sts. rem. for each shoulder. Leave sts. on a holder.

LEFT SLEEVE:

Work as for Right but dec. on p. rows.

TO MAKE UP:

As for Lady's Sweater.

COLLAR:

Using no. 10 needles pick up sts. around neckline, right side facing and adjust on first row to 126—132/136—140 sts. Work 5 ins. in k.1, p.1 rib. Cast off ribwise. Join Left seam and collar. Press all seams. Fold collar on to right side.

CIRCULAR KNITTING METHOD

LADY'S SWEATER

BODY OF SWEATER:

Using circular needle no. 13 and Mc. cast on 224—238/252—266 sts. and work 2 ins. in k.1, p.1 rib. Change to circular needle no. 10 and st.st. (k. all rds.). When entire work measures 15½—16/16½—17 ins. complete the border patt., from chart, beg. as indicated. Cont. in Mc. On next rd. shape armholes.

Size 34 and 36: K.3 sts., place a marking thread here and regard this as beg. of rds.

x Cast off 7—8/8—9 sts., k.98—103/110—115, cast off 7—8/8—9 sts., place another marker here. x Rep. from x—x. Leave work aside.

SLEEVES: (Both alike.)

Using set of needles no. 13 and Mc. cast on 58—60/64—66 sts. and work the welt as before. Change to set of needles no. 10 and st.st. Inc. 2 sts. at underarm, 1 st. either side of the first and last st. of rd. every 8th rd. until there are 97—99/103—107 sts. When entire sleeve measures 17—17½/18½—19 ins. shape armhole. Cast off 7—8/8—9, k.83—83/87—89, cast off 7—8/8—9 sts. Place sts. on an extra needle.

YOKE:

Using circular needle no. 10 k. the work on to same in the following order. K. Back, beg. at first marker, Sleeve, Front, Sleeve. N.B. On first rd. k. tog. the first and last st. where each piece meets. Place a marker at each to denote where to dec.

RAGLAN SHAPING:

x K.1, slip 1, k.1, pass the slip st. over, k. to the last 3 sts. before the next marker, k.2 tog., k.1 st. x Rep. from x—x 3 times. (Dec. 8 sts. in all). Dec. likewise every third rd. 18—19/13—14 times, then on alternate rds. 9—9/18—18 times. 142—144/142—148 sts.

COLLAR:

Using set of needles (or short circular needle) no. 10 regulate the sts. on first rd. to 140—142/144—144 sts. and work ½ inch in k.1, p.1 rib. Then turn the work inside out. K.14 rds., p.1 rd., k.2 rds. and work the first 14 rds. of border patt. Cont. in Mc. k.2 rds., p.1 rd., k.7 rds. for facing. Cast off.

TO MAKE UP:

Darn in all loose ends. Omitting ribbing press work on wrong side with a hot iron over a damp cloth. Allow to dry. Fold collar facing on to wrong side and slip st. Press lightly. Join at underarms.

MAN'S SWEATER

BODY OF SWEATER:

Using circular needle no. 13 and Mc. cast on 256—270/270—282 sts. and work 2 ins. in k.1, p.1 rib. Change to circular needle no. 10 and st.st. (k. all rds.). Place a marker at beg. of rd., another after 128—135/135—141 sts. to denote sides. Inc. 1 st. at each marker every 8th rd. at alternate sides of same until there are

280—294 / 294—308 sts. When entire work measures 12—13/13—14 ins. work the first 39 rds. of border patt. then shape the armholes. x Cast off 10—10/10—11, k.120—127/127—132, cast off 10—10/10—11 sts., place a marker here. x Rep. from x—x. Leave work aside.

SLEEVES:

(both alike)

Using set of needles no. 13 and Mc. cast on 60—60/64—66 sts. and work the welt as before. Change to set of no. 10 needles and st. st. Inc. 1 st. on first rd. Further inc. 2 sts. at underarm, 1 st. either side of the first and last st. of rds. every 8th rd. until there are 91—91/97—99 sts. When entire sleeve measures 13½—14/14½—15 ins. work the first 19 rds. of border patt., inc. likewise every 6th rd. until there are 97—97/103—105 sts. Work the next 20 rds. of patt., beg. as indicated., inc. likewise every 4th rd. 109—109 / 115—117 sts. Then shape the armholes. Cast off 10—10/10—11, k.89—89/95—95, cast off 10—10/10—11 sts. Place sts. on an extra needle.

YOKE:

Using circular needle no. 10 k. the work on to same in the following order. Back, beg. at first marker, Sleeve, Front, Sleeve. N.B. On first rd. k. tog. the first and last st. where pieces meet. Place a marker at each to denote where to dec.

RAGLAN SHAPING:

x K.1, slip 1, k.1, pass the slip st. over, k. to the last 3 sts. before next marker, k.2 tog., k.1 st. x. Rep. from x—x 3 times. (Dec. 8 sts. in all). Dec. likewise every third rd. 9—7/13—11 times Then on alternate rds. 27—30/25—28 times. 126—132/136—138 sts.

COLLAR:

Change to set of needles (or short circular needle) no. 10 and work 5 ins. in k.1, p.1 rib. Cast off ribwise.

TO MAKE UP:

As Lady's Sweater. Fold collar on to right side.